Creepiness

Creepiness

Adam Kotsko

Winchester, UK
Washington, USA

First published by Zero Books, 2015
Zero Books is an imprint of John Hunt Publishing Ltd., Laurel House, Station Approach,
Alresford, Hants, SO24 9JH, UK
office1@jhpbooks.net
www.johnhuntpublishing.com
www.zero-books.net

For distributor details and how to order please visit the 'Ordering' section on our website.

ISBN: 978 1 78279 846 0
Library of Congress Control Number: 2014945879

A CIP catalogue record for this book is available from the British Library.

Design: Stuart Davies

Printed and bound by CPI Group (UK) Ltd, Croydon, CR0 4YY

We operate a distinctive and ethical publishing philosophy in all
areas of our business, from our global network of authors to
production and worldwide distribution.

CONTENTS

Acknowledgments

I would like to begin by thanking Natalie Scoles, who has been a constant help with this trilogy since my first tentative drafts of *Awkwardness* and whose insights not only sharpened my argument and expanded my range of examples, but helped keep me motivated and energized to complete this book. I could wish for no better partner—in conversation, in life, and in endless TV marathons.

I must also thank Anna Kornbluh, who responded in detail to multiple drafts from the earliest stages of this project. Her incisive critiques pushed me to revise, expand, and rethink my argument in countless ways. She is a true friend and intellectual comrade.

Many others helped me along the way, including: Eric Santner, who conducted a summer seminar that helped me to grapple with Freud in a way that proved absolutely decisive for the shape of this project; Sean Andrews, who invited me to speak at Columbia College in Chicago and commented on an early draft; his students and colleagues at Columbia, whose questions and comments in the question and answer session and at the pub afterward made important contributions to my thinking on creepiness; my students and colleagues at Shimer College, whose responses to my talk there pushed me yet further; Beatrice Marovich, who provided crucial insights into the history of the TGIF programming block; Ian Petrie, Ben Robertson, Karl Steel, and other Twitter correspondents, who reminded me of the most salient aspect of the Fonz's creepiness; the pseudonymous blogger "Voyou," whose post on *Spring Breakers* deeply shaped my interpretation of the film; and Brad Johnson, who helped me to refine my (almost certainly correct) prediction about the ending of the Netflix series *House of Cards* and who put up with incessant online chat sessions about my writing process. My thanks to all of them, and to the countless friends, acquaintances, barbers, bartenders, and total strangers who have shared their thoughts on creepiness with me over the years.

Finally, my profound thanks to Tariq Goddard, who generously found a place for *Awkwardness* at Zero Books and who has been an invaluable advocate of my work since then. I am honored to be a part of his remarkable series.

The specter of creepiness

Beginning in the mid-2000s, the fast food chain Burger King began running a series of deeply disturbing advertisements. They star a revamped version of the company's mascot, The King, who has left the world of animated children's advertisements and is now played by an actor wearing a large plastic mask featuring a crown, a beard, and an alarming perpetual smile. One typical ad features a man waking up in the morning to find The King in bed with him, staring at him inches away from his face. The man is initially alarmed, but becomes calm when The King hands him a breakfast sandwich. As he eats, he and The King become friendlier, joking, laughing, and even briefly brushing hands—and then they both flinch away and face forward in the bed. In another, a man wakes up, opens the blinds, and finds The King standing there staring at him. He starts to become agitated until he notices that The King is holding a plate with a breakfast sandwich.

This ad series, whose mascot was widely called the "Creepy King" in the press and among viewers, generated considerable word-of-mouth attention for Burger King, and in a sense it could be viewed as one of the most successful "viral marketing" campaigns of all time. Unfortunately for Burger King, the attention was almost uniformly negative. My father, one of the most easy-going people I know, at one point asked if I had seen the ads and expressed genuine outrage that Burger King was trying to sell hamburgers using homoerotic voyeurism.

Other viewers were similarly repelled, and the firm's advertising agency, Crispin Porter + Bogusky, tweaked the formula slightly. In one later ad, The King crashes through an office window in a relentless quest to replace a woman's microwaved lunch with a huge hamburger, while in another he engages in a "reverse pick-pocketing" scheme wherein he sneaks money into people's pockets, apparently symbolizing his commitment to saving customers money. One ad reprises the home invasion theme by casting The King as a member of a group of buddies sneaking into their friend's room to wake him with a blow horn. This more overtly masculine take on the character was continued in a series of ads in which The King is digitally inserted into classic hockey matches.

The shift to surrealism was not enough to shake the "Creepy King" image, and ultimately the mascot was retired. Yet The King lives on, seared into the American cultural consciousness as an enduring archetype of creepiness. I've been researching the topic for years, primarily by asking people what they think of creepiness. Every definition I attempt is rejected as inadequate, and every creepy pop-cultural character seems open to other interpretations—except for one. The King is the one example that always receives unanimous consent.

Doubtless a big part of the character's impact is the simple shock that such an off-putting theme would be part of an advertisement. It's rare enough to have an aggressively creepy character on television, and even then the writers will normally make some effort to make the character somehow relatable or sympathetic. Yet The King has no back-story, no mitigating factors. He is sheer creepiness embodied, all the more so given his unexpected irruption into a genre that normally makes every effort to pander to the viewer.

How could this happen? On a practical level, one can see how a space for such an unprecedented campaign could open up precisely at Burger King. A perpetual also-ran in the fast food industry, Burger King is a frequent target for private equity companies eager to snatch up ailing firms and apply their cost-cutting magic to return them to profitability. Hence it is also a chronically mismanaged firm, lurching from one contrived strategy to the next. In that context, an advertising campaign that used shock value to generate cheap publicity could easily sound like a plausible option.

It seems to me, however, that there is a deeper truth at work in the "Creepy King" campaign. This truth emerges in one of the least creepy King ads, which portrays him breaking into McDonald's headquarters to steal the recipe for the Egg McMuffin so that Burger King can produce a copycat sandwich. Here we have a company openly admitting to its own redundancy, its lack of any mandate for existence. Maybe Burger King can give you slightly more food, or give it to you cheaper—but at the end of the day, it's not contributing anything distinctive, original, or even particularly desirable. The commercials in fact exacerbate this sense of providing a generic food substance by referring to Burger King's food primarily as "meat," rather than naming the particular type of meat involved. Finally, the use of the mascot only highlights the contrast with McDonald's: while we might imagine people being nostalgic about characters like Ronald McDonald or the Hamburglar, literally no one has fond memories of the old Burger King mascot that this ad is reviving.

There's no reason for me to have any emotional connection with Burger King beyond the minimal investment it takes to prefer a Whopper to a Big Mac—and yet these commercials are manipulating me into a very strong (if negative) emotional response. As unprecedented as this ad campaign is on one level, though, is it really anything more than an intensification of what has been latent in Burger King all along? Haven't all of its ads made disproportionate emotional demands on us, asking us to feel some kind of loyalty or affection for a McDonald's knock-off? Burger King has nothing to offer us, and yet it has been demanding our attention and shoving itself at us nonetheless. In the last analysis, there was always something creepy about Burger King, and for a brief, uncanny moment, they were honest about it.

From the uncanny to the creepy

During my career as a commentator on popular culture, it has become clear that I am doomed to live out my jokes. My first book in this trilogy, *Awkwardness*, grew out of a pub discussion where I used Heideggerian terminology to describe awkward humor, claiming that awkwardness was "a fundamental attunement of Dasein." The more I thought of it, though, the less it seemed like a joke—and eventually I was forced to actually write a book on it. The idea for a sequel initially came up as a joke as well. Having recently learned that one of my colleagues was planning to write a trilogy of books—a project of which I was, shall we say, a bit skeptical—I told my girlfriend: "If he can write a trilogy, so can I! Awkwardness, creepiness... and sociopaths!"

As I will try to show later in this introduction, this trinity of social dysfunction was not accidental, but was dictated by the terms of the very trends I was trying to diagnose. This same inner logic drove me to initially skip past creepiness, following up on *Awkwardness* with *Why We Love Sociopaths*—the time was not yet ripe. Perhaps a wiser man would have stopped there, yet I remained haunted by creepiness, unable to give up on the idea even though I found it in many ways unappealing.

I am not the first commentator to be drawn almost involuntarily into the territory of creepiness. Most notably, Sigmund Freud beat me to it by nearly a century, in his 1919 essay "The Uncanny" (available, among many other places, in a Penguin Classics collection of which it is the title essay). The term "uncanny" is a translation of the German word *unheimlich* (literally "unhomely"), which refers to a wide range of phenomena associated with fear and dread. Freud detects an ambivalence in the term, which etymologically seems to refer to what is unfamiliar (what we are not at home with) but experientially most often involves something that is *all too* familiar, something that fits *too well*.

Here we can see the appropriateness of the English translation "uncanny," which we might invoke to describe a coincidence or an unexpected resemblance. Most of Freud's examples, however, involve horror at the supernatural, which is not a context where we would normally use the word "uncanny." And indeed, Freud surveys various European languages and concludes that there is no language other than German that unites the various meanings of *unheimlich* in a single term.

Looking over Freud's suggested possible translations of *unheimlich* into English, however, I wondered whether we have finally caught up with the Germans in this regard. Collected from various dictionaries, they include "uncomfortable, uneasy, gloomy, dismal, uncanny, ghastly; (of a house) haunted; (of a man) a repulsive fellow." Today, we do have a single word that encompasses all of those meanings: "*creepy*," which is associated at once with ghosts and the supernatural, with vaguer forms of discomfort, and with particularly off-putting individuals like The King.

As Freud explicates his examples, drawn mostly from horror stories, he focuses on the unexpected persistence of beliefs that the individual or society as a whole are supposed to have outgrown. On the individual level, Freud claims that many uncanny experiences derive from exaggerated childhood fears of punishment by one's father, most notably the threat of castration. On the broader social level, it is a question of certain "primitive" beliefs about the power of the dead, which scientific modernity should have wiped out but which still remain just beneath the surface.

This leads Freud to endorse the definition of the philosopher F.W.J. Schelling, who declares that "*unheimlich* is the name for everything that ought to have remained hidden and secret and has become visible." Freud is thinking primarily of disavowed beliefs, but Schelling's definition would also include the sexual creepiness that comes to the fore in the Burger King ads as well as in everyday use of the term. We can see this perhaps most clearly in the case of neurotic young men who are mortally afraid of being declared creepy. At bottom, they fear that if they reveal their sexual desire, it will provoke a reaction of revulsion and disgust—better to keep it hidden, then.

The sexual roots of the English word "creepy" go back to around the 1600s, when the term "creep" was used to describe thieves, particularly those who robbed customers in brothels. This note of invasiveness seems to go back to the primary meaning of the verb "to creep," referring to the locomotion of insects, who are always undesired intruders into the home. Interestingly, however, by the middle of the 1800s, the term began to refer not to an outside agent, but to the unexpected behavior of one's own body, as in the idea of a "creeping in the flesh"—hence the shift of "creepy" into the realm of horror movies, which produce goose bumps. And in 1849, Dickens coined the idea of "the creeps," describing the feeling produced by various forms of creepiness in abstraction from its particular cause.

Admittedly, the translation of *unheimlich* as "creepy" may initially seem to stretch the category beyond the bounds Freud sets out in "The Uncanny." Yet insofar as it introduces an element of sexuality, it does so in a fundamentally Freudian way. Freud's account focuses on social expectations, particularly in the form of paternal prohibitions, and for Freud those phenomena are inextricably tied up with sexuality. In fact, although the common understanding of Freud views him as focused on the individual psyche, I believe that his theory is better understood as an attempt to account for the fraught relationship between sexuality and the social order. And this is because Freud is above all concerned with understanding how human beings deal with what we could call *the inherent creepiness of sexuality*, with its tendency to transgress and evade all reasonable boundaries.

Freud believes that the psyche responds to two different kinds of stimuli: external and internal. The external are relatively straightforward: they arise, we respond, and it's over. The light is too bright, so I turn away. A bug is biting me, so I swat it. Even if the stimulus keeps coming back, each instance can be viewed as a more or less isolated incident—it's always possible to imagine a particular stimulus never coming up again.

One could think that the same would hold for internal stimuli, which we might think of as something like animal instincts. I get hungry, so I eat. I have an itch, so I scratch it. These stimuli will of course eventually come back, but in the meantime, I can go about my business. Yet Freud claims that things are not so simple. Our internal stimuli are certainly related to simple bodily needs, but transposing them into the mental realm has an unintended side-effect. Bodily needs are inherently finite, but when they are transformed into mental representations, into *ideas*, they slip loose of any physical curb or limitation.

On the physical level, I want to eat to satiate my hunger, but transforming hunger into an abstract idea allows it to become strangely detached from its ostensible goal: I just want to *eat*, period. Freud maintains throughout his career that the most productive way to think about these desires is through the lens of sexuality, which is the most unruly desire of all. We can envision animals getting an urge to mate, finding a partner, and then going about their business as though nothing had happened. For human beings, though, sexuality can potentially suffuse every aspect of life—and the ostensible goal of repro-duction is, as a rule, far from our minds when we are obeying our sexual urges.

What Freud is presenting us with, then, are desires that are *inherently* excessive. It's not that, for instance, there is a proper amount of food I should be eating and I cross the line into eating too much. Rather, in Freud's account of the human psyche, excessive desires detached from any determinate goal or boundary actually *come first*.

In order to differentiate these urges from simple animal instincts and to emphasize their compulsive character, he calls them "drives." All of human life for Freud is an attempt to manage these inescapable, unruly desires. Everything that comes more or less naturally for animals (at least as we tend to imagine or idealize them) is a laborious achievement for human beings. The challenge of somehow emerging from the process of development as a coherent self with a manageable range of desires stems in part from the fact that we can't always get what we want—we must negotiate our way through the obstacles of physical reality and social prohibitions if we are to find some form of satisfaction. Yet the problem is more fundamental than that: all these unruly desires don't simply conflict with physical and social reality; they also conflict *with each other*. Satisfying them all is *inherently* impossible, even given the most hospitable circumstances.

What we might view as "normality" is actually only a comparatively sustainable strategy for holding things together in the face of these inescapable, mutually contradictory urges. All of our strategies, however, have unavoidable drawbacks and unintended consequences. For instance, in the course of development, most human children come to "internalize" social expectations in some way, which works well as a strategy for reliably avoiding actions that result in punishment. This internal representative of the social world is what is known as the "superego," which stands over the "I," watching and assessing its every move. Yet Freud's clinical experience showed him that once they become internalized, those social demands can become just as relentless and unruly as any other internal stimulus or drive, leading to intense feelings of guilt and an actual *desire* for punishment.

The most aggressive strategy for dealing with our unruly desires is what Freud calls "repression." It occurs when a desire is so unacceptable to us that recognizing it would shatter our sense of who we are. When such a desire threatens to surface, we force it deep into the unconscious mind, never to return. Our drives are clever, however, and they will seek every opportunity to make their demands felt. They are also flexible, willing to take what they can get—whether that means being vicariously satisfied through another closely related drive, or even taking a completely inverted form. Our aggressive, destructive drives, for example, can be satisfied through the superego's aggression toward *us*. For Freud, the sadist and the masochist are mirror images, and he continually vacillates over which, if either, should be considered the "primary" form of which the other is the inversion.

When we turn to the topic of psychological disorders, then, it's clear that they can't be viewed as deviations from some kind of pre-existing norm. Our drives are *inherently* deviant to start with. As the psychoanalytic theorist Alenka Zupančič puts it in her recent book *Why Psychoanalysis?*, Freud's theory of drives shows us that "human sexuality is a deviation from a norm that doesn't exist." Rather than appealing to some abstract standard or norm, Freud's concern is whether the balance struck between the demands of the drives, the external world, and our societies' expectations is livable and sustainable.

Creepiness, sexuality, and society

With this in mind, I would like to provisionally support my claim that Freud's theory is about the inherent creepiness of human desire. First, to summarize, for Freud human desire is inherently excessive, and for the "normal" subject, repressed desires can be experienced as unwelcome and invasive when they threaten to resurface. Desire is also willing to displace itself into seemingly unrelated realms or point itself in counterintuitive directions, making it very difficult to interpret and understand—indeed, there is a sense in which desire is fundamentally and irreducibly enigmatic. Finally, Freud puts forward sexuality as the privileged point of reference for understanding all desire and claims that our relationship with social norms is always inextricably tied up with our struggle with sexuality.

Accepting for the moment that The King is a particularly potent figure of creepiness, we can see that these properties of desire—its displaced, invasive, excessive, and enigmatic character, along with the special role of sexuality and social norms—are all emphatically present in the advertisements. There is something undeniably sexual about the early "Creepy King" commercials, because he is, after all, crawling into other men's beds and staring into their bedroom windows. The commercial I described in detail makes the implicit homoerotic tension explicit when the man and The King touch hands only to flinch away, so that the social expectations surrounding the proper performance of heterosexual masculinity are very much in play. The relationship cannot be consummated, and so the sexuality is displaced onto the breakfast sandwich or other fast food items. As a result, the sexualized sandwich is strangely fetishized as the camera lingers on it, so that the aforementioned references to "meat" seem to emphasize the *fleshiness* of the food in a creepy way.

This displaced sexual energy is both invasive and excessive. The King is first of all an unwelcome, disturbing presence in the home, but he is constantly invading other personal spaces too— the break room at the work place, even people's pockets. Even in the less overtly creepy commercials, he is constantly breaking the rules, as when he invades a hockey game or breaks into McDonald's headquarters. One begins to get the sense that The King somehow "gets off" on the very act of transgressing rules and boundaries, regardless of the context.

The King's invasion is generally not for the purposes of stealing, however, but precisely of giving something extra, whether it be fast food or extra money. Often the excessive size of the sandwich in question is highlighted, but there is something especially appropriate about The King's association with fast food breakfast, which is inherently excessive regardless of its size. For most Americans, a fast food breakfast is an exceptional indulgence, most often reserved for road trips or used as a kind of nuclear option to cure particularly painful hangovers. In this context, the dollar or so that The King shoves into people's pockets as a result of Burger King's lower breakfast prices can also appear excessive, insofar as it represents "savings" on something that relatively few people would normally buy.

Perhaps the creepiest aspect of The King, however, is his mask. Were a normal actor, even a creepy one like Zach Galifianakis, to appear in some unsuspecting customer's bed, the effect would presumably be less alarming. This is because the static facial expression renders The King's motives completely illegible. When he reveals that all he wants is to deliver a breakfast sandwich, the enigma of his desire is not so much dispelled as redoubled—why on earth would anyone want to do that? Is he trying to make friends? Is the breakfast sandwich poisoned? Or laced with some kind of date-rape drug?

What's more, in The King the Freudian properties of unruly desire are all deeply intertwined. There is something excessive, for instance, about a sexualized relationship with a sausage and egg biscuit, and that displacement makes the desire involved seem much more enigmatic than a simple desire to eat breakfast. Meanwhile, it somehow fits that The King should literally invade people's personal space, as the sexual desire at work is already figuratively "invading" realms where it does not belong.

The King is perhaps unique in so clearly exemplifying all these aspects of unruly desire, but I contend that all of them will be involved to some degree in any creepy experience. Admittedly, the place of a particular property may not be immediately clear. For instance, in the case of a sleazy guy who insists on propositioning every woman he meets, the element of enigma may seem to be missing insofar as he clearly wants sex. And yet it seems strange that simply wanting sex would be creepy, because a man who politely asks a woman on a date and then accepts the answer is, all things being equal, not being creepy. What makes the sleazy guy creepy, then, is not that he is simply asking too many women out, but that his constant failure seems to indicate that he *doesn't care* that his methods are ineffective. It's as though he's directly "getting off" on the very act of approaching women, with no regard for the ostensible goal of sleeping with them. When we recognize this, we can't help but ask, "What is he *getting* out of this?" Even the most seemingly obvious creepy desire turns out to be enigmatic on closer examination.

By the same token, a single creepy property, if strongly expressed, can give rise to the entire ensemble. Something like this seems to be going on in the trope of the "creepy uncle." In a society where the nuclear family is emphasized above all, relationships with extended family members can easily become confusing and even illegible. It's simply not clear what to do with an adult male who is "family," but also not one's father. This ambiguity can be productive in some cases like the "cool uncle" or the "confidant uncle" — but the possibility of reading the uncle's motives as invasive or enigmatic is ever present. Is the "cool uncle" using his nephews and nieces as a chance to relive his childhood? Is the "confidant uncle" prying into my secrets for less than pure purposes? And is it just me, or did that hug last a little bit too long?

There are obviously many tragic cases where uncles take advantage of their role to abuse their young relatives. Yet that empirical fact is not enough to account for the emergence of the "creepy uncle" as a cultural trope, since abuse by fathers is much more frequent and there is no widespread stereotype of one's own father as creepy. It is the uncle's displaced and enigmatic role as "family but not *really* family" that opens up the space for other creepy tropes to attach to the figure of the uncle in a way that is not really possible for a more clearly defined role like that of the father.

To return to the territory of "The Uncanny," however, there is a broader sense in which the father—in his role as the representative of social expectations—*can* become creepy, and that is when the father's voice and perspective invades the subject's own psyche and begins making excessive demands. Freud believes that this sense of an outside agency inside of oneself, watching over one's every move and criticizing it, is what accounts for the uncanny effect of doppelgangers—or, I might add, the creepy feeling of discovering we are being watched. This is why it was creepy, for instance, when it was widely reported in the press that the algorithm that tracked a young woman's purchases at Target deduced that she was pregnant before she knew it herself.

Yet who exactly is *doing* the "creeping out" here? While this may be an extreme case, our common experience of creepiness always tends to complicate questions of agency to some degree. We speak primarily of "being creeped out," and when we reverse that passive expression into the active voice to say that someone or something "is creeping us out," we don't usually mean to imply that they are doing so intentionally. Indeed, creepy people's obliviousness to the way their behavior comes across is often an integral part of the creepy effect. Further, as the Target example shows, no conscious agency needs to be presupposed—we can be creeped out by corporations, by places, by inanimate objects, even by periods of time (who is not vaguely creeped out by the 1970s?). We hesitate to say that these things are *inherently* creepy, and yet the judgment that something is creepy seems somehow more than simply "subjective." We know that we're a party to this judgment, that to some extent we must be projecting, but we can't say exactly why or how.

The Target example is a particularly striking one because here there appears to be some kind of agency involved even though there was no human agent at work. A computer simply observed a certain pattern of purchases, compared them to other customers, and started recommending further purchases, with no understanding of what it might all mean. This sense of a non-human or mechanical agency is another area that Freud designates as uncanny, since it seems to imply a secret or hidden form of agency beneath the recognizably human surface. Freud believes that this accounts for the creepiness of witnessing an epileptic seizure or other forms of compulsive action like Tourette's syndrome.

When we use the concept of creepiness to expand Freud's analysis of the uncanny to include sexuality, we can understand why incidents involving inhuman agency would be *unheimlich* in Freud's sense of hitting a little too close to home. We all have such hidden agencies roiling beneath the surface of our official public persona, made up of our unruly drives, our social expectations, and—most troubling of all—their mutual entanglements. We are susceptible to being creeped out, in other words, because we are always in danger of being creeped out by *ourselves,* or more precisely, by those parts of ourselves that seem to exceed and elude us.

Hopefully, at this point, I have made an initial case that Freud's account of the inherent unruliness of the drives provides helpful conceptual tools for understanding the complex dynamics of creepiness. Yet for me, what is most convincing about this approach is not the detail that Freud helps us to account for, so much as the way he allows us to answer the more fundamental question: why would we watch creepy characters? Many theories could likely account for what is off-putting and repulsive about creepiness, but few could account as elegantly as Freud's for why creepiness is also fascinating: because it is fundamentally about our struggle with desire and sexuality.

The inertia of white masculinity

This is not the first time Freud has suggested himself as a point of reference in my study of popular culture. Although my hope in *Why We Love Sociopaths* was to stick more closely to the pop-cultural texts as a way of making up for indulging excessively in Heidegger in *Awkwardness*, I found myself consistently drawn to familiar Freudian concepts like the Oedipus complex in describing what was going on in the shows I analyzed.

Here I plan to follow that approach more systematically, using Freud's diagnostic categories as a typology of creepy characters. Given Freud's reputation as a sexist, patriarchal thinker (mostly exaggerated, though in part deserved), this approach may seem unfortunate, or even a step backwards compared to my previous books. Early critics of *Awkwardness* critiqued me for failing to account for women's experience of awkwardness. I tried my best to remedy the problem in *Sociopaths*, where there were more women, as well as people of color, available to use as examples. This makes sense, given that sociopath narratives are so often about social climbing—and while sexism and racism remain very much alive, in recent decades more space has opened up for individual women and people of color to get ahead in the world.

In retrospect, it's clear that the lack of women's experience in *Awkwardness* stemmed from my overly narrow focus on the most recent trend in awkward humor, which was initially dominated by white men. If I had written the book even a few years later, there would have been many more examples focused on women's experience (a circumstance that is in large part due to the same kinds of feminist critiques that my book faced).

Yet while this shift toward women's awkwardness may seem to be a new trend, in a very real sense it's merely a return to normal. Women's comedy has always been about awkwardness, most often the awkwardness of a young single woman in the workplace or else of being a young married woman feeling her way into the role of wife and mother. Mary Tyler Moore played both roles in her long career, first as Dick van Dyke's awkward spouse and then as the awkward career woman in her eponymous series. One thinks too of *I Love Lucy*, or *Golden Girls*, or *Sex and the City*—in fact, once we notice the connection between awkward humor and women as lead characters, it's hard to think of a counterexample.

The interesting question for me, then, is exactly why the "awkwardness trend" was initially so male-dominated—to the point where it blinded even an avid TV viewer like me to the long-standing dominance of women in the field of awkward humor. I believe the explanation is that many white men felt unsure of their social position in light of white women's increasing independence and success in previously male-dominated fields and especially in light of the changing expectations that reality had created for romantic relationships. A critical mass of white men were open to the claim that "men are the new women"—and hence an appropriation of women's distinctive mode of humor, based on a feeling of being perpetually out of place, seemed like a plausible move.

This same insecurity also gave rise to the fantasy of the sociopath, who was often exaggeratedly masculine (Tony Soprano) when he wasn't literally inhabiting the "simpler days" of clear gender roles (Don Draper). Though it may initially seem odd that the shows growing out of this white man's fantasy include many more women and people of color, the contradiction disappears when we note that it is most often white men who recognize the promise of the subaltern striver (as in Don Draper's elevation of Peggy Olsen, or in Stringer Bell's belief that hobnobbing with white developers made him more than a simple gangster). It's all of a piece with the idealization of white male dominance: "See, we're open-minded! Having us in charge isn't so bad!"

Hence, without being initially aware of it, I have been writing a kind of internal critique of white masculinity under the conditions of late capitalism. The fact that it is ending up in the quagmire of creepiness is not simply a result of living out my own joke, however—it is strictly dictated by the inner development of the pop-cultural materials themselves. It's obvious enough that awkward men are afraid of being judged creepy, which was why creepiness sprang immediately to mind as the second item in my joke trilogy.

More surprising is the intimate link between creepiness and the sociopath fantasy. I noted in *Why We Love Sociopaths* that most sociopath-centered shows follow the same basic pattern: first they induce you to identify with the amoral anti-hero, and then over time they start to punish you for having made such a terrible amoral decision. What has struck me as I've watched the concluding seasons of "high quality cable dramas," however, is how often they punish the viewer precisely by portraying the hero as a creep. I will discuss this at more length in later chapters, but hopefully two brief examples will suffice for now. An obvious one is Tony Soprano, who in later seasons murders a close associate and then leers at the deceased's widow as she breast-feeds her newborn son. Even the serial killer Dexter somehow manages to become creepier by the end of his run, embarking on bizarre incest plots whose creepiness is compounded by the fact that the actors playing Dexter and his besotted sister got married and divorced during the course of the series.

If anything, this trend confirms that the sociopath is indeed the fantasy of the awkward white man in particular, who fears creepiness above all. What was perhaps unexpected, however, was that as the sociopath trend began to wane, we witnessed the emergence of a trend where creepiness is openly embraced, as in the comedy of "Tim and Eric" or the film series *The Hangover*. If I had attempted to do a study of creepiness as early as five years ago, when I began this series, it would not have worked—there simply were not enough good pop-cultural examples. Now, however, there are plenty.

Here it might be worth returning to the "Creepy King." I

suggested at the beginning that there was an underlying creepiness to Burger King's continued existence, given that they don't seem to contribute anything original or desirable to human society. They're simply there because they've always been there. The same may be said of the company's primary target audience, which its annual reports from the period describe as the "hungry guy" demographic. While the ads themselves are studiously diverse in their casting, it is difficult to understand this phrasing as anything but a euphemism for "white guys." And—to say nothing of their role in political and economic life—aren't white guys essentially the Burger King of the pop culture world? A handful are doing very creative work, but for the most part, they give us nothing but endless sequels and remakes while gratuitously alienating other groups even when it cuts against their own economic interests.

The time when the experience of white, straight, middle-class men could put itself forward as representative of an identifiable "mainstream" has long since passed, and yet they persist. Further, no one can seriously believe any of the past ideological justifications of white male dominance. They are not the exemplars of universal justice. They are not the vanguard of democracy. They are not even the model for technological advancement or economic growth. And yet here they are, still in charge of almost everything.

In the face of this situation, they tried the self-pity of awkward humor, but now women have retaken the lead in what was always their own territory anyway. With somewhat greater success, they tried the paradoxical idealization of sheer ruthless power in itself. While the sociopath genre produced some of the greatest television shows of all time, it has now fizzled out into the pointless sadism of *Game of Thrones*. And now—as we're living under the first black president, who will most likely be followed by the first female president, and as the Chinese seem poised to take the lead in technological and economic growth—

we finally arrive at sheer creepiness for its own sake. With no possible justification for their own persistence, white straight men fall back on their last pathetic refuge: "I may be a pathetic creep, but *at least I'm honest!*"

In many ways, this trend shows white straight men at their worst and most self-involved. It is at best incurious about people of other races and sexual orientations, likely due to the widespread belief among white straight men that black and gay men are effortless seducers. At worst, it indulges in casual homophobia and racist stereotypes. It is by turns denigrating and idealizing of women, presenting them as easily manipulated, as ungrateful, or else as geniuses with ninja-like physical abilities. It is dominated by a strange nostalgia for the cheap consumer detritus of the 80s and 90s, to the point where simply *mentioning* an obscure toy is supposed to count as a joke. All this is of course in addition to the inherent repulsion of creepiness itself.

Creepiness and culture

Yet I watch, and I don't think I'm alone. There's something compelling about creepiness, even something attractive. I saw it already in my research—never once did my questions about creepiness fail to produce animated, impassioned discussion from those I asked—and I also saw it in the response to my public talks and in the frequent exhortations that I *had* to write this book. We reject and revile creepiness, and at the same time, we want it. My goal in this book is to figure out why, and my contention is that the ongoing collapse of white straight male culture—for all its many unappealing qualities—represents a unique opportunity to thoroughly explore the question.

Freud's work is uniquely situated at the intersection of the universal element in creepiness and the contingent forms it takes in the white straight male culture whose decline I am documenting. I don't mean to say, as Freud often seems to do, that the specific patriarchal cultural patterns he diagnosed are themselves universal in any sense. While he was admittedly overconfident in jumping to such conclusions from his observations of the strategies people used to cope with it, I believe his account of the basic problem of desire hit on something that has a much better shot at true universality.

Many are understandably distrustful of any form of universality, but I think it's worth the risk to consider whether something like the unsolvable deadlock between the drives, the external world, and social norms might be a problem that confronts every human individual and every human community. More traditional Western notions of universality tended to envision some kind of positive norm like the ideal of perfect justice. This sounds very nice, but in practice, traditional universals most often become an excuse for castigating (and, where possible, dominating) other societies for failing to live up to the objective standards that Westerners conveniently just happen to exemplify. In Freud's theory of the drives, by contrast, what is truly universal is the radical lack of any norm, any reliable standard of measurement, any permanent solution. What's universal isn't some transcendent truth to which only a few have access—it's the fact that, at the end of the day, none of us knows what the hell we're doing.

At the same time, Freud's specific diagnostic categories fit extremely well into "mainstream" (white straight male) popular culture, and it's easy to understand why this would be the case. Freud's milieu in Vienna was in many ways strikingly similar to the white middle-class American milieu of the 1950s and 60s, which remains such a constant point of reference for mainstream popular culture. His account of the ways that unruly desires could become unmanageable was based on his observations of people who had been raised in patriarchal nuclear families where any sexual indulgence outside the boundaries of heterosexual marriage was considered destructive and shameful—in other words, in a structure broadly similar to what we know as the so-called "traditional American family."

Broadly speaking, we can say that Freud recognizes four basic ways in which our drives can overcome our defenses and begin running astray—that is to say, four ways in which the primordial creepiness of the human being can reemerge between the cracks of our social selves. These include the two forms of neurosis (hysteria and obsession), along with perversion and psychosis. I should emphasize that there is no category for the "normal." Even our most workable strategies are always in danger of collapsing into one of these disorders—the difference between health and illness isn't so much the underlying psychological structure, but whether a sufficiently strong force has managed to disturb it.

A "healthy" person is always predisposed toward a certain mental illness, or to put it differently, a healthy person is afflicted with that disorder in a livable rather than a pathological way. Hence Freud could claim that in his social setting, most people were neurotics, and that differences in the way male and female children were generally treated tended to turn men into obsessives and women into hysterics. This does not mean that every individual is suffering from unmanageable symptoms, but that if things eventually did break down, they would break down along those particular lines. In reality, even someone with a structural predisposition toward psychosis, the most serious and debilitating form of mental illness in the Freudian scheme, can live something like a normal life more or less indefinitely.

As I noted above, I will use these diagnostic categories as a kind of typology of creepy characters. My intent is not to "diagnose" the characters as though they were real people, but rather to show how they conform to certain ideal types. This approach also fits with the spirit of psychoanalysis itself, which regards each patient as ultimately unique in the way his or her personal history has shaped them (which always means:

misshaped them), so that diagnostic categories can represent only a kind of shorthand or initial indication of the direction of treatment. And indeed, as we will see, the categories apply not only to individual characters, but to the structure of the shows themselves, to the ways they solicit and presuppose the viewer's desire.

The most extreme disorder, and the one where Freud enjoyed the least success in his attempts at treatment, is **psychosis**. In the battle between their drives and the external world, psychotic subjects choose a particularly radical solution: they totally reject reality and construct "their own little world" in accordance with their desires. Often this world maps onto the real world sufficiently for the psychotic subject to function, but the correspondence is fragile and easily disrupted—and once it is broken, it can be extremely difficult to reestablish. In everyday terms, the psychotic form of creepiness is what we experience when we're around someone who appears to be "crazy." Our unease is not simply a response to that person's seeming unpredictability, but our discomfort in the face of a person for whom *we don't exist*— fundamentally, nothing the psychotic does has anything to do with others.

The next category is **perversion**. The perverse subject tries to resolve the conflict between desire and social prohibition by "officially" acknowledging the rules while still maintaining some small, unrepressed outlet for the prohibited desire, most often some kind of fetish-object or fetish-behavior (such as voyeurism or exhibitionism). In extreme cases, social norms themselves can become fetish-objects, so that the subject feels entitled to carry out the most immoral acts precisely in the name of morality—and it is from this perspective that we can understand many sociopathic characters as they make the shift into creepiness.

Freud found perversion and fetishism fascinating and believed they had important insights to offer psychoanalysis, and yet, much to his chagrin, he found that fetishists rarely sought out psychiatric help. This was because they did not view their fetish as a problem, but instead straightforwardly embraced it as something that made them happier and more functional. Hence the perverse character often evinces a profound self-assurance that can be very attractive to someone who is paralyzed by awkwardness.

The final two categories are subsets of **neurosis**, which happens when the subject totally submits to social expectations and represses unacceptable desires. As I already noted, in Freud's observations the two versions tended to fall out along gender lines, with male children turning out obsessive and female children turning out hysterical—and that's generally how things work on television as well. Even though changes in child-rearing practices and gender norms have loosened this connection considerably in the real world, the connection is much stronger in the realm of television, which tends to rely on broad cultural stereotypes even in our supposedly enlightened age.

In **obsession**, the subject gets caught between two equally strong but incompatible desires, one socially acceptable and the other not. While he or she normally succeeds in repressing the unacceptable desire, in pathological cases it keeps managing to resurface, leading the subject to engage in compulsive behaviors that are meant to act out a disavowal of the undesirable desire. The "awkward man" who is creeped out by his own sexuality is a perfect example of the obsessive neurotic.

Where the obsessive is caught between two desires that are relatively straightforward in themselves, the **hysteric** suffers from a fundamental lack of clarity as to what it is the social order is demanding of him or her. It is difficult to think of a modern example of the type of pathological cases that Freud dealt with in his practice, which resulted from the extreme thwarting of female desire in what is misleadingly called "traditional marriage" and which normally manifested themselves through psychosomatic symptoms. Under contemporary conditions, it seems more common for the hysteric to react to the irreducible conflict of desire by essentially opting out of desire altogether. This desire gone on strike can be the creepiest of all, prompting observers to ask their own hysterical, unanswerable question: "What do you *want*?"

This typology does not directly correspond to those put forth in my previous books, but broadly speaking, neurotic characters belong to the terrain of *Awkwardness*, while most of the characters analyzed in *Why We Love Sociopaths* belong in the categories of psychosis and perversion. In what follows, I will devote a chapter to each diagnostic category, using specific examples to flesh out the ways that desire goes awry in each case—and more importantly, to explore the ways that each variant of creepiness manages to produce its own peculiar power of attraction.

Chapter I

Their own little world

Creepy main characters have historically been almost unknown on television, and even today they remain a relatively rare phenomenon. Yet creepiness has often been close at hand in the form of the creepy neighbor. Even in television's most conservative era, the figure seemed to be irresistible, as shown in *Leave It to Beaver*'s slimy Eddie Haskell, a manipulative schemer who appears to have sexual designs on Mrs Cleaver. Over time, there was a marked tendency for creepy side characters to take over the show. This is arguably what happened on *Happy Days*, where "the Fonz"—a grown man who spends all his time hanging out with teenagers and repeatedly refers to a public restroom as his "office"—quickly became the main draw of an otherwise standard family sitcom.

An even clearer example is the strange case of *Family Matters*. The show seems to have begun as a variation on *The Cosby Show*, focusing on a working-class African-American couple and their upwardly mobile, college-bound children. The true star, however, is the nerdy next-door neighbor, Steve Urkel, an accident-prone mad scientist with an obsessive love of the family's oldest daughter, Laura. Originally intended as a one-time guest star and so initially more a sight-gag than a genuine character, Urkel talks in a whiny, nasal voice and wears excessively tight clothing. Most alarmingly, he always walks pelvis-first, the rest of his gangly body struggling to keep up.

At least until the advent of The King, Urkel was perhaps the single clearest example of televised creepiness. He is invasive, constantly dropping in on his neighbors unannounced. His desire is both enigmatic and excessive: exactly what is it that he likes about Laura, and why does he persist after literally a decade of constant rejection? Perhaps creepiest of all, it gradually becomes clear that his apparent attraction for Laura is actually a displaced expression of his desire to be part of his neighbors' loving family. Ultimately, the most impassioned relationship of the show is not that between Urkel and his juvenile crush, but the bromance *avant la lettre* between Urkel and his neighbor Carl Winslow, a middle-aged police officer and father of three.

As the show wears on, Urkel collects additional creepy baggage, including an ability to transmute into a suave seducer named Stefane Urquelle through self-administered genetic alterations. Perhaps creepiest of all, however, was the growing gap between the age of the actor—who was in his early teens when the show started and his early twenties by the end—and the perpetual adolescence of his character.

Family Matters began as a spin-off of *Perfect Strangers*, where the mother from the former show had first appeared as a sassy elevator operator. A variation on the *Odd Couple* premise, *Perfect Strangers* is centered on the conflicts between Larry Appleton, a mild-mannered Chicago reporter, and his cousin Balki Bartokomous, a recent immigrant from the remote island of Mypos. A strange amalgam of Eastern European and Mediterranean stereotypes, Balki speaks with a thick accent, mangles American cultural norms, and frequently celebrates his good fortune with an elaborate and embarrassing "dance of joy." The theme of the show is essentially what happens when the creepy neighbor moves in with you—and as it turns out, it's not so bad, as the otherwise unimpressive Cousin Larry receives a major boost to his social life and embarks on a wide range of improbable adventures.

What's particularly interesting to me, however, is the way in which Balki's overwhelming presence distracts from the fact that Larry himself is a perfect candidate for a creepy neighbor. As a docile bachelor who has difficulty expressing his emotions, he has a marked predilection for dating women who live in his own apartment building. Ultimately he and Balki wind up pairing off with two attractive roommates, but it is easy to imagine a show told from the two women's perspective, in which Larry is the sad-sack neighbor who's always looking for an excuse to knock on their door and leer at them. In an uncanny foreshadowing of the current creepiness trend, it appears that the only way to defuse creepiness is to redouble it.

Both *Family Matters* and *Perfect Strangers* were staples of the ABC network's long-running programming block TGIF, a series of family-oriented sitcoms that ran on Friday nights. For my family as for many in the late 1980s and early 90s, TGIF was "appointment television." We watched it religiously, even when the shows were in reruns, and we marked the occasion by indulging in the special treat of ordering pizza or getting fast food.

Looking back, *Family Matters* and *Perfect Strangers* were hardly the only TGIF series to be defined by creepiness. Surely the worst offender was *Full House*, the story of Danny Tanner, a widower and father of three girls, who does Cousin Larry one better by inviting *two* creepy neighbors to move in with him and "help out" with things. Uncle Jesse, a wannabe rock star who goes through a series of unfortunate haircuts, is at least Danny's brother-in-law, but Uncle Joey, a struggling stand-up comic, isn't even related to Danny or his daughters. In later seasons, the creepiness is compounded when Uncle Jesse marries and the couple continue to live with the unconventional family while making thinly-veiled jokes about their active sex life in front of the children.

Not satisfied with the inherent creepiness of the show's premise, the *Full House* writers threw in a creepy neighbor. In an interesting variation on the theme, this time the creepy neighbor is a girl named Kimmy Gibbler, who is the best friend of the oldest daughter, DJ. She shares Steve Urkel's invasiveness and desire to join her neighbor's family, but whereas Urkel had one obsessive love, Kimmy's interests are more diffuse and promiscuous. With a self-assurance far beyond her years, she draws attention to herself through her garish dress and frequently propositions men, most notably Uncle Jesse.

Kimmy is presented as unattractive—on both a visual and an olfactory level, as her horrendous foot odor is a running gag—and personally obnoxious, and hence her sexual desire is treated as inherently excessive and out of place, even aside from her age. Perhaps the creepiest episode to feature Kimmy, however, is one in which the men of the house envision their future. In the fantasy scenario, Kimmy, whose future is irrelevant to the plot and whose appearance in the episode is thus totally gratuitous, is played by a sexy adult actress in a slinky black dress. Emphasizing this sexualization of their teenage neighbor, when Danny asks the group what they've learned from their glimpse into the future, Uncle Joey responds that he has learned he should be nicer to Kimmy Gibbler. In another episode, Uncle Jesse has a nightmare about his pathetic future in which he is married to Kimmy, who appears dressed like the overly sexualized Peg Bundy of *Married... With Children*.

The show thus presents both uncles sexualizing Kimmy—and in both scenarios, what is strangely overlooked is that she is the same age as the young woman whom both men treat as a daughter. Here the timeless tropes of the creepy neighbor and the creepy uncle are seamlessly intertwined, in one of the most successful family sitcoms in history. The question that haunts me now is whether we loved these shows despite their creepiness, or—as now seems more likely—because of it.

What does a creepy neighbor want?

The creepy neighbor is usually played up for laughs, but when the writers begin to explore the characters on their own terms, they inevitably wind up in very dark places. This is clearest in the case of Steve Urkel, whose parents are neglectful and even abusive toward their son. One particularly vivid example is an episode that portrays him spending Christmas in his cold basement laboratory with his parents nowhere to be found, but many episodes make it clear that the Urkels are ashamed of their oddball son and are not afraid to let him know. Things are less disturbing in the case of Kimmy Gibbler, but her parents make it clear that she is unwelcome in her own home, in one case punishing her by grounding her—to the Tanners' house.

It might initially seem strange that the writers would feel a need to explain why a teenager would be spending a lot of time away from home. Adolescence is the time of life when building connections to one's peers is the most important priority, whether that be strong friendships or romantic relationships. It is thus possible to imagine a best friend character, or a boyfriend or girlfriend, whose omnipresence is simply taken for granted, without any need for a back-story or explanation. This seems to be the case with the best friend character on *The Wonder Years*, for instance.

Yet neither Urkel nor Kimmy fits this pattern. Though Kimmy is DJ's best friend, she also takes a strong interest in the adult family members, which is not normally the case for teenagers. And Urkel, of course, is constantly rebuffed in his romantic advances, so that he's less a boyfriend than a stalker. Instead of trying to find their place within the peer group apart from their family, both characters are trying to form surrogate family relationships, albeit not with the same level of urgency. It's as though their initial family somehow didn't "take."

In Freudian theory, this kind of failure of the familial bond is what gives rise to psychosis. This is because, for Freud, what is at stake in our initial social bonds is more than a matter of physical survival—our earliest relationships structure our very relationship with reality. It is in the context of our family that we develop a sense of our own identity, and the family serves as a kind of "home base" for our developing relationship with the broader social world. (Freud strongly emphasized the mother's role in the former task and believed that the father had a special part to play in providing a kind of conduit between the family milieu and society at large. However, for our contemporary context, I would emphasize the importance of the actual developmental steps themselves rather than the gender of the person who is primarily responsible for them.)

In short, if one's initial family doesn't "take," one's relationship with reality doesn't "take" either. Deprived of a real gut-level relationship with our shared social world, psychotic subjects create "their own little world," which often bears a close enough resemblance to the real world to allow them to function on a day to day basis. Even in the most successful cases, however, the psychotic's desires and motivations will always appear to be somehow "off," somehow askew relative to what is recognized as normal behavior. What's more, there is generally no way to make the psychotic person understand where they are misfiring — within the coordinates of their own private world, their actions make perfect sense. As in Freud's essay on the uncanny, there is an agency at work here, but it is an unrecognizable form of agency that doesn't take account of us. Hence the creepiness of the psychotic character, whose enigmatic desire seems to invade our world from elsewhere.

It is in this context that we can understand the often delusional behavior of the creepy neighbor. Given that Steve Urkel's family alienation is most intense, it makes sense that his behavior is strangest. Even after a decade of rejection, he believes that he is making progress in his courtship of Laura, frequently claiming, "I'm wearing you down!" Though he is incredibly clumsy, he seems unaware of the fact, responding to the often catastrophic effects of his mishaps with his characteristic catchphrase: "Did I do that?"

Most alarming of all are the Stefane Urquelle episodes, which appear to involve some kind of psychotic break. But while one might initially see this persona as evidence of multiple personality disorder, in reality it is simply an intensification of what Urkel is trying to convince himself is already happening—he's found a shortcut to winning Laura's heart, but he would have won her over eventually in any case. And it cannot be an accident that the transformation comes from Urkel's genetic self-manipulation, the most aggressive and literal way of disavowing his family heritage and replacing it with another.

Other creepy neighbors fit this pattern as well, to varying degrees. They may have their own elaborate system of responding to social situations, such as Balki's reliance on the cultural mores of the made-up nation of Mypos. They may develop elaborate moral codes that do not match up with the realities of their setting, like the Fonz. Or they may simply be radically self-assured in the absence of any socially recognized justification for their confidence, as in the case of Kimmy Gibbler.

As I said in the introduction, falling into a certain diagnostic category in Freud's schema does not mean that one is non-functional. Every psychological structure is ultimately an elaborate coping strategy, and though some may seem to be more inherently robust than others, each one provides the subject with at least some chance at a livable life. For the more light-hearted psychotic neighbors on television, part of that coping strategy is to find supplemental emotional support to make up for the initial lack in their family bonds.

Returning to the question of whether my family was attracted to the TGIF line-up despite or because of its creepiness, it might be helpful to reflect on the paradoxical narrative role of the creepy neighbor. On the one hand, the writers are constantly asking us to scapegoat and deride the creepy neighbor's unattractive characteristics and inappropriate behavior. On the other hand, though, doesn't the creepy neighbor serve as a point of identification? After all, the viewer is always implicitly intruding into the private space of this fictional family's home, and the characters are traditionally presented as an idealized family that everyone might want to be part of. In other words: *we viewers are the ultimate creepy neighbors*—hence the special fascination of creepy neighbors, which often allows them to take over the show entirely. And what better setting for a creepy neighbor than a house that turns out to be full of creeps?

Creepy, scary, spooky

Depictions of creepy neighbors frequently distinguish a subset who do not avail themselves of this intrusive strategy, choosing instead to be quiet and keep to themselves. I am speaking, of course, of the very creepiest of creepy neighbors: serial killers. Instead of investing their libidinal energy in attempting to establish some kind of relationship with the broader world, they opt for a destructive rejection of that world.

In *Why We Love Sociopaths*, I talked at length about the example of Dexter, who was deeply traumatized when he witnessed the horrendous death of his mother. When his adoptive father realized Dexter was unable to control the resulting violent impulses, he embarked on an ambitious two-pronged solution to the problem. On the one hand, he developed a series of rules known as The Code that made sure Dexter would only murder people who deserved to die but had escaped legal judgment based on some kind of technicality. On the other hand, he trained Dexter to project an image of bland conformity so that he would never draw attention to himself. In reality, all pop culture serial killers arrive at a similar approach to their destructive drives, developing a highly ritualized code for who they kill and what they do with the bodies and otherwise remaining beneath the radar as much as possible. What makes Dexter unique is only the "moral" nature of his Code and the explicitness with which it was imparted to him.

The serial killer can help us get at the difference between the closely related concepts of creepiness and scariness. To put it briefly, what makes the serial killer scary is that he is going to kill you—but what makes him creepy is that he is not really killing *you* at all. The person caught up in the serial killer's ritual is playing a role in the serial killer's world that bears no necessary relation to the victim's own identity in the social world most of us share.

We might say that scariness is about physical threats, whether real or imagined, whereas creepiness is threatening at a more diffuse level of abstract desire. The two can often go together, as in the exemplary case of the serial killer, and that's because the possibility of being scared by a purely imagined threat makes it ultimately impossible to draw a firm line between them.

It is in the overlap between the scary and the creepy that we find the spooky. Ghosts are by definition invasive, intruding into the realm of the living where they don't belong. Further, like the creepy neighbor, they most often invade precisely the realm of the home. The classic ghosts who have unfinished business are not exactly psychotic, given that they are deeply invested in a particular social world and the obligations it lays upon them— but it is still "their own little world" insofar as it is a world that has passed and that thus has no bearing on the shared experiences of the living. In addition to being invasive and displaced, the ghost's desire is excessive in that it grants an eternal significance to events and circumstances that for the living person would often seem to be fairly commonplace and insignificant— and of course the ghost is enigmatic, with the narrative thrust of ghost stories usually centering on deciphering what it is that the phantom wants.

The close relationship between creepiness and spookiness is what has allowed for the proliferation of eroticized supernatural creatures. Vampires have always been a site of erotic fantasy, but they have surged in popularity in recent years, both on television and in young adult fiction. The television show that most embodies this trend is *True Blood*, where vampires "come out of the coffin" and try to live among humans as peers. The vampire lifestyle is of course very different from normal humans, given that they are immortal, can only reproduce by sucking a human being dry and converting them into a vampire, and of course need to drink human blood to survive. (The latter need is obviated by the development of the artificial blood substitute from which the show takes its name, but few vampires actually embrace veganism in practice.)

While there is a ridiculously elaborate back-story that includes a wide array of other supernatural beings, *True Blood* is most interested in sexual relationships between vampires and human beings, which stand at the intersection of scary (is the vampire going to drain me completely?) and creepy (what exactly is the vampire getting out of this relationship?). This overlap may also account for the popularity of supernatural romances aimed at teenage girls. After all, sex is scary for all young people, especially those who are in danger of becoming pregnant, and the motives of teenage boys are often as inscrutable (and potentially as malevolent) as those of a vampire.

The enigma of Adult Swim

The broad Freudian category of the psychotic thus embraces a wide range of characters. All of them are alienated from the social world, albeit for different reasons, and they react to this alienation differently. The extreme poles are the creepy neighbor, who seeks to rejoin the social world by establishing a surrogate family bond, and the serial killer, who plays on social expectations as a cover for his attempt to actively destroy external reality. Supernatural creatures are variations on the theme. Unlike the creepy neighbor or serial killer, "their own little world" is not purely personal, but it is foreign to the shared social world of living human beings.

Hence in *True Blood*, for example, vampires may act as either creepy neighbors who want to join our world or else as serial killers who want to destroy it—and yet this does not seem to exhaust the field. There is a third option of isolationism, of withdrawing into the vampire culture and minimizing contact with human beings. The shape-shifters and werewolves portrayed in the show's ever-proliferating subplots most often embrace this strategy of hibernation. In ghost stories, too, no matter how destructive or friendly the ghost may be, the end goal is almost always to find a way to get the ghost out of the human world and back into their own ghostly realm.

Is there any equivalent to this strategy of withdrawal outside the supernatural realm? At first glance, it may not seem like a formula for compelling television, but one of the most remarkable features of the current creepiness trend is the emergence of a nightly programming block devoted to various psychotic "little worlds." I am speaking, of course, of Adult Swim. This spin-off grew out of a series of attempts to attract older viewers to the youth-oriented Cartoon Network in the evenings. Early on, offerings catered to adult viewers with serious nostalgia for the cartoons of yore, with much of the programming initially devoted to anthology shows that compiled shorts from the golden era of Looney Toons.

The program that proved most influential for the future direction of Adult Swim, however, was *Space Ghost Coast to Coast*, a mock talk show that debuted in 1994 and was "hosted" by Space Ghost, an obscure superhero drawn from 1960s Hanna-Barbera Saturday morning cartoons. While the show did have live-action guests, they were only part of a surrealistic brew that consisted primarily of the host bickering nonsensically with other cartoon characters from his era. I vividly remember stumbling across this show as a teenager and being strangely transfixed by the show's very incomprehensibility (which was enhanced by the fact that the guest for that evening was Björk, who was actively playing along with the craziness).

Beginning in the early 2000s, several other shows inspired by *Space Ghost Coast to Coast* debuted. Most of them drew their characters from the same Hanna-Barbera "universe" as *Space Ghost*, a seemingly counter-intuitive move given that Hanna-Barbera cartoons were generally more cheaply produced and less popular than those coming from Disney or Warner Bros. Yet this focus on second-tier, forgettable childhood TV was perfectly calibrated to tap into viewers' nostalgia, which would be triggered all the more powerfully by the shock of recognizing something they had not consciously thought about for years if not decades.

Even if they looked the same, however, these did not seem to be the same characters we watched on lazy Saturday mornings. Like Space Ghost, they had changed in important ways, becoming more petty, more violent, more nihilistic—and much more creepy. In place of the often convoluted plots of the original cartoons, Adult Swim shows were openly free-associative, showing the characters to be motivated primarily by a desire to overcome their pervasive boredom. They weren't so much stories as misfired comedy sketches that persisted long after their concept had been exhausted. In light of the fact that such non-narratives are more difficult to sustain, the shows typically used a 12-minute format, allowing for four different shows to appear in rapid succession during a traditional one-hour programming block.

These shows go beyond merely portraying psychotic characters. They seem to be psychotic in their very structure, off in "their own little world" with no necessary relation to the viewer's. The use of animation rather than live-action reinforces this separation from the normal world.

At this point, my readers may be wondering why anyone would watch such a thing. The answer is that, at least according to conventional wisdom, the majority of viewers were drunk or high. Though I have never been a pot smoker, I first encountered the Adult Swim block at a get-together with a group of friends who were. The detached state produced by marijuana seemed to allow them to enter into the shows on their own terms, reacting purely to isolated events without any attempt to stitch them together into a larger whole.

Even without the requisite chemical stimulation, though, I was intrigued, particularly by one of the few classic Adult Swim shows that does not rely on old Hanna-Barbera characters: *Aqua Teen Hunger Force*. The title and the opening credits seem to promise us the adventures of a team of superheroes based on fast food items. Yet our heroes—Master Shake (a huge anthropomorphic Styrofoam cup), Frylock (a floating box of French fries with a goatee), and Meat Wad (who is much as one would expect him to be)—do little other than sit around their squalid house and bicker with each other.

In other words, creators of *Aqua Teen* have taken the Adult Swim format and done it one better, creating their own third- or fourth-tier superheroes to engage in pointless non-adventures. The use of fresh animation also allows them to try an innovative format, recording semi-improvised dialogue and only animating the characters' speech afterward. The result is uncanny in that the Aqua Teens seem strangely more alive and real than most animated characters, despite their ridiculous appearance. More specifically, they seem like a group of early adolescent boys left to their own devices. Frylock is the older brother who is losing interest in childish things—he has an elaborate scientific lab and a powerful computer—but can still be drawn in. Master Shake is the kind of mischievous kid who gets most of his ideas from TV, constantly hatching nonsensical schemes and claiming to have engaged in sexual exploits despite clearly not knowing what sex actually consists of. And Meat Wad, as befits the malleability of his physical form, is the younger brother who is perilously vulnerable to bad influences (as in his frequent claims that he is going to try "hardcore crack").

On one level, then, *Aqua Teen* is an exploration of what happens to a bunch of latchkey kids who are essentially on a perpetual summer vacation, so that the setup itself resonates strongly with many viewers' own childhood experiences of binge TV-watching. On another level, though, it is a kind of redoubling of the creepy neighbor scenario, insofar as the Aqua Teens are creepy neighbors to their own appallingly creepy neighbor, Carl. A fat, bald, unemployed man, Carl is the subject of constant harassment, not least because—in another poignant echo of summer boredom—he has a mostly unused swimming pool in his back yard. His only pleasures in life are overeating (at one point he raves that after taking advantage of an all-you-can-eat buffalo wings deal, he'll be "farting blood") and pornography (which is invariably playing on his big-screen TV whenever the Aqua Teens barge in on him).

In any other series, Carl would be an object of derision, but here he becomes strangely sympathetic. He is constantly subjected to horrific violence, often suffering torture and dismemberment in a grim parody of cartoon characters' ability to die and then return unscathed. His association with the Aqua Teens has left him outside of the law's protection—he claims at one point that the police have stopped answering his calls—and hence outside of human society. Carl is seemingly content to remain in his "own little world" of unemployed squalor, but the Aqua Teens have very forcefully pulled him into theirs. Hence he may exist as a kind of parody of the Adult Swim viewer himself, who is at least minimally pathetic in that he's watching cartoons late into the evening rather than dating or socializing with friends.

Adult Swim is far from the first cultural product to explore the theme of escaping into the world of television. Indeed, this concept produced one of the most enduring monuments of creepiness: the film *Cable Guy*, in which Jim Carrey's titular character worms his way ever deeper into a cable subscriber's life. This character, who belongs alongside The King and Steve Urkel as one of the archetypal creeps, was a neglected child whose only comfort was television. As a result, he spends his adult life enacting idealized TV tropes about friendship and family by attempting to spend every waking moment having adventures with his newfound "friend" and becoming a de facto member of his family.

One of Adult Swim's most popular programs, *Robot Chicken*, takes the opposite approach, inviting viewers to relive their childhood isolation. Like many young boys who came of age before the advent of video games, I spent hours upon hours playing with "action figures" (i.e. posable dolls mainly based on cartoon and comic book characters), spinning elaborate plots in which they mostly killed each other repeatedly. In *Robot Chicken*, those action figures quite literally come alive through the magic of stop-motion animation. The scenarios, which sometimes last only a few seconds, mostly ask the viewer to ponder what it would be like if action figures had to join the adult world. Their very first sketch is exemplary (and arguably remains their best). Here, Optimus Prime, the leader of the Transformers, has to interrupt repeated adventures in order to urinate. Over time, it becomes clear that he has a serious problem, and when he goes to the doctor, he receives a diagnosis of terminal prostate cancer. His fellow Transformers all tearfully huddle around his hospital bed as he dies—and then "transforms" into a coffin.

What *Robot Chicken*'s procedure highlights is that many of these cartoon characters and toys already ostensibly belonged to the adult world. In *G.I. Joe*, to pick just one example, the opposing teams of G.I. Joe and Cobra were not simply the representatives of good vs. evil; they were also bureaucratic institutions with their own office politics and even love triangles. Hence it's not much of a stretch when another *Robot Chicken* segment portrays the Emperor from *Star Wars* receiving a phone call from Darth Vader informing him that the Death Star has been destroyed—and interrupting the Lord of the Sith to take a call from the person who's picking up lunch from the deli for everyone at the office.

In addition to its original programming, Adult Swim has often taken on "cult hits" that were cancelled by other networks. One example is *Futurama*, which relies on *Robot Chicken*'s strategy of transposing cartoon characters into adult settings. The show is a science fiction parody set in the distant future, with all the attendant alien races and advanced technology—but it centers on the employees of a cut-rate delivery service and their petty problems.

Adult Swim's most successful rescue, however, is *Family Guy*. As I discussed in *Why We Love Sociopaths*, this show imitates *The Simpsons*, which presents the cartoon father as an impulsive child with adult powers and privileges. The real innovation of *Family Guy*, however, and what probably made it such a good fit on Adult Swim, is its use of brief "cut scenes" that have nothing to do with the plot. Most often these snippets refer to old cartoon shows or other pop culture trivia from the 80s and 90s, and from one perspective they obviously undermine the coherence of any given episode. Yet if we step back and view the main plot and the cut scenes together, we can see that for the *Family Guy* writers, the sitcom tropes that structure the main story exist on the same level as any other pop-cultural reference.

In other words, in the *Family Guy* universe, the idealized sitcom family is no longer some kind of compensation or aspiration, but exists as a seamless part of the "little world" of childhood fantasy. The sitcom dad is just as available for manipulation and recombination as the action figure. On one level, this intermingling reflects my own experience during summer vacations: I was just as happy to watch reruns of *Golden Girls* as to watch any explicitly kid-oriented show. In fact, without any point of reference for the "real" adult life of which the sitcoms formed an exaggeration and idealization, the shows' characteristic tropes and gimmicks took on a life of their own, akin to the rules I had to learn to understand other fictional universes.

Once sitcoms are shorn of their ideological authority—as a lens for understanding and evaluating one's own family life and as a utopian ideal to be aspired to—it becomes clear how strange and creepy so many sitcom tropes really are. This is one way of understanding the casual racism and sexism of *Family Guy*. Though it has long since devolved into a lazy "provocativeness," it likely began as a way of pushing the Adult Swim strategy to an extreme and asking what it would be like if people *really* lived like they do on sitcoms. At the root of this cynical knowingness, however, there is a deep force of nostalgia—not for the authentic family life that classic sitcoms hold up as an ideal, but for *the sitcom itself*, simply as such.

The shift from *The Cable Guy* to *Family Guy* is the shift away from trying to live out TV fantasies in the real world and toward attempting to live *inside* the TV fantasy, with no reference to the real world whatsoever. Once this shift has taken place, popular culture is no longer part of a shared social world, but becomes raw material for constructing a psychotic "little world" to withdraw into.

Don Draper as creepy neighbor

It is here that I would like to turn, perhaps unexpectedly, to *Mad Men*. I already analyzed the show at length in *Why We Love Sociopaths*, but here I would like to focus on the sixth season, which aired in the summer of 2013. Together with an intensive study of Freud that same summer, watching this disturbing, emotionally draining season of *Mad Men* was what convinced me that I finally had to write the present book—because week by week, I was witnessing Don Draper, the very archetype of the charming sociopath, descend into the abyss of creepiness.

In many ways, the sixth season seemed like a completely different show. This is clear on the immediate visual level, where the seemingly timeless fashions of the late 50s and early 60s are slowly being displaced by the trends of the 70s, which often appear cheap and seedy in retrospect. While the shifting fashions are dictated by the show's historical period, it's hard not to see this move toward the 70s—widely acknowledged as the creepiest decade on record—as a visual foreshadowing of the creepiness to come.

Don's behavior remains in many ways the same, and yet it all feels somehow "off." His obligatory adulterous affair doesn't feel like a necessary escape or even a tormented passion. Instead, it feels pathetic and desperate. It is riskier, insofar as he is now sleeping with his downstairs neighbor, and it is also more gratuitously hurtful, given that he is not only betraying his young second wife but is also cuckolding a neighbor who has become a good friend. His impulsive business decisions (to drop an important client and to merge with a rival firm) no longer seem bold, but both inconsiderate and ill-considered. And in his relationship with his young protégé, Peggy Olsen, the old combination of sternness and appreciation is replaced by manipulation and petty interference in her sex life.

The season is marked by a heavy reliance on flashbacks to Don's adolescent years. Previous seasons had revealed that he was the son of a prostitute who died in childbirth, a fact that his abusive father and adoptive mother never allowed him to forget. When his father was kicked in the head by a horse and died (an event the young Don witnessed), his foster mother took Don to live in a whorehouse run by her brother-in-law. On their first night there, he witnessed his uncle extorting sex from his foster mother, who was heavily pregnant with the younger brother whom Don would later drive to suicide by shunning him. Subsequently, Don lost his virginity (not entirely of his own free will) to a prostitute who was caring for him during a serious illness, and when his foster mother found out, she beat and denounced him for his shameful behavior.

This is surely a remarkably screwed up childhood, and it's no wonder that Don jumped at the chance to assume his present identity when fate and a North Korean bombing raid conspired to make it possible. It's a dream come true—almost as though Urkel had found a way to live permanently as Stefane Urquelle! In the present context, we can also see that this kind of thorough-going alienation from one's family is a seedbed of psychosis. Yet where are the delusions?

Here I would like to point out that the many "flashbacks" of Don's past are often very explicitly *visions* that are appearing to him. Most commonly, figures from Don's past appear in his contemporary setting. At the end of the fifth season, for instance, the suicide of a close friend prompts a series of visions of his younger brother, another victim of suicide, who at one point engages Don in a lengthy conversation. Another example comes at the beginning of the third season, when he has an elaborate vision of the mother he never met as he is boiling milk for his own new baby—and he is so engrossed that he burns the milk. Sometimes the flashbacks might seem to be memories triggered by a similar event in the present, but even in those cases, someone has to interrupt the vision to get him to "snap out of it."

Viewers have often complained of the overuse of flashbacks, particularly in the sixth season, believing them to provide an overly simplistic explanation or even excuse for Don's behavior. If we view Don's personality as psychotic in structure, however, what the flashbacks mostly explain is the existence of the flash-backs themselves. And in fact, what is so remarkable about Don as a character is that his behavior is usually *not* explained or determined by his past. One clear case comes at the end of the third season, when a vision of his father's death seems somehow to inspire him to found a new agency to escape a contract that would crush his creativity. We know in retrospect that the result of his father's death was that he was taken to live in a whore-house by a reluctant foster mother who resented him—and he responds to the vision by interrupting that sequence and taking control of his own circumstances. In the sixth season, by contrast, he increasingly wallows in his past. What has changed?

Perhaps the most famous scene in *Mad Men* is Don's Kodak Carousel pitch, where he delivers a powerful meditation on nostalgia accompanied by a slide show of his own family photos. The most interesting thing about this scene, as I discussed in *Why We Love Sociopaths*, is that he buys his own pitch—he had previously begged off spending Thanksgiving with his family, but now he rushes home to join them, only to find that they've already gone. This scene confirms the viewer's perspective that Don has very consciously tried to construct the idealized family for himself and yet views himself as fundamentally an outsider who needs to force his way in. In other words, Don is a creepy neighbor *to his own family*. The writers confirm this by creating an uncanny double for Don in the form of an actual creepy neighbor kid named Glen, who is alienated from his divorced mother and believes Don's wife Betty to be a beautiful damsel in distress (an assessment that is not entirely inaccurate).

When Don's family falls apart by the end of the third season, he spends much of the fourth wallowing in his childhood shame, at one point hiring a prostitute on Thanksgiving to slap him repeatedly in the face for being such a bad boy. He only pulls himself together when he marries his secretary, a woman who seems to combine effortless motherliness with all the ambition and creativity that attracted him to his mistresses. As a result, he pulls off an unprecedented full season without committing adultery—although not without a disturbing fever dream in which he murders an old fling who seduces him and then threatens to tell his new wife. The creepy neighbor has finally joined the idealized family, and he's ready to become the serial killer to protect it.

Don's good behavior proves unsustainable, and soon he has taken up with Sylvia, a woman who lives as close as possible to his own home. He then proceeds to try to turn her into his whore. At one point he gives her money after he has overheard her husband refuse to do so, and most disturbingly, he puts her up in a hotel for a day and unfolds a bizarre domination scenario in which he explicitly tells her that she exists only for his sexual gratification. She understandably breaks off the relationship after that, and he then spends a drug-fueled night trying to develop the perfect advertising strategy to win her back. Later, they briefly reconcile, and in one of the most devastating scenes of the entire series, Don's daughter Sally walks in on them—he can't even protect his children from his shame. At the same time, his wife's acting career begins to take off, leading to her performing sex scenes that he regards as whorish. All of this follows on a storyline in the previous seasons in which the partners of the advertising agency quite literally whore out their office manager, Joan, to win a client.

Thus the entire world that Don has so carefully constructed is turning into yet another whorehouse. The strategy of the creepy neighbor is spent, as there is no remaining idealized family to join, and so he must find another approach. We might interpret his capricious business decisions as a violent acting-out akin to that of the serial killer, but his dominant strategy is one of withdrawal into "his own little world" —and, as in *Robot Chicken*, that world is ultimately the world of things.

This strategy of withdrawal seems to come to a head in the final episode of the series, when Don delivers a disturbing pitch to representatives of Hershey's, a potential new client that has never run any kind of advertisement before. Reducing the room to stunned silence, he tells them that an occasional Hershey's bar (which he earned by stealing money from johns in the brothel, making him a creep in the strict etymological sense) was his one joy in a childhood otherwise filled with shame and deprivation, and actually discourages them from advertising at all, as the meaning and appeal of their product will always be immediately apparent to every young boy.

The effect is chilling—and thoroughly creepy to his business associates. His revelations are excessive and out of place in a business setting, and he seems to imagine a close relationship with the new clients as representatives of Hershey's, making the pitch invasive as well. Most importantly, though, his reasons for making such a self-destructive pitch seem irreducibly opaque to the people around him. Don's partners in the firm quickly move to expel the creep from their midst, putting him on indefinite leave. The season ends with Don taking his children—notably, on Thanksgiving Day—to see the dilapidated brothel where he grew up. Here, as in the Hershey's pitch, his motives are enigmatic to his children, so that the whole season ends on a note of ambiguity.

On one level, this season of *Mad Men* is the most thorough example of reducing one's hero to a creep in the history of the sociopath genre. Yet the writers don't simply leave the audience there. The moments that might initially seem most creepy—his Hershey's pitch and his presentation of the brothel to his children—in fact represent Don's effort to pull off the near impossible and restore his connection to reality. Up to this point, both his business life and his family life have been based on lies, which have sometimes been exposed by individuals but never become "public knowledge." As that fantasy begins to collapse in a more comprehensive way in this season, he understandably retreats into himself for a time—but then he takes the radical step of trying to integrate all the pain he's been repressing into his social world, represented by his workplace and his children. With his "own little world" in ruins, he dares to reestablish the connection to reality that he initially refused.

It is relatively clear what brought Don to this point, but the question that now arises is how he was able to get so far in life in the first place. As I've mentioned before, according to Freud's theory, many people with an underlying psychotic structure should be able to put together a "little world" that matches up closely enough with the shared social world to allow them to function—but not all of them become high-powered advertising executives and multi-millionaires with their pick of attractive women.

The writers imply that he developed early the skill of ingratiating himself with strangers, but I think a big part of the answer is simply that Don Draper is *really, really good-looking*. In this sense, arguably the best commentary on *Mad Men* is an episode of *30 Rock* where Liz Lemon dates an incompetent airhead portrayed by the actor who plays Don Draper, Jon Hamm, whose handsome appearance causes people to treat him as though he's a brilliant surgeon and a professional-level tennis player.

People are willing to collaborate in constructing Don's "little world" because they are attracted to him—but it's not just a matter of an attractive surface. If Don Draper's descent into creepiness corresponds to something like a psychotic break, his psychotic structure also accounts, on a more fundamental level, for people's attraction to him. They can sense his freedom, his lack of any real investment in social norms. This is what allows him to promote a talented young secretary to copywriter, or boldly start a new ad agency, or impulsively marry a young aspiring actress who views herself as his equal.

We might say the same about the structure of the show itself, which relies, like its main character, primarily on its attractive surfaces. Indeed, perhaps the most consistently perceptive commentary is the "Mad Style" series written by the bloggers Tom and Lorenzo, which interprets the episodes and characters based primarily on wardrobe choices. Like Don Draper's "little world," *Mad Men* presents us not so much with a full picture of the social milieu of the 1960s as with a facsimile built out of objects and snippets of advertising. When "real world" details—such as the legal ramifications of the new agency started at the end of season three—get in the way, they are simply ignored.

At least as important as the framing of the time period, however, is the show's own increasingly elaborate sequence of references back and forth among plot points, images, and individual lines of dialogue. Each season is almost like a Talmudic commentary on previous ones, creatively reinterpreting prior episodes in a way that enriches their meaning. What could easily have been a perfunctory period drama actually allows itself remarkable freedom in shaping, and continually reshaping, its own distinctive world.

This freedom has allowed the show to transform itself radically over the course of its run, even taking the bold risk of becoming harsh and difficult to watch as it traces its main character's descent into a creepy despair—and so, to that extent, the very shift into the deviant sixth season anticipates Don's own escape from his psychotic self-enclosure.

This same radical freedom is also what lets the creepy neighbor take over an innocuous family sitcom, what allows us to be so strangely fascinated by serial murderers, and what gives even the self-indulgent escapist fantasies of Adult Swim cartoon shows their bizarre attractive force. Here creepiness is not something to be shunned or hidden, but a source of profound power and liberation. For the psychotic, all things are possible— and yet all things are simultaneously unbelievably fragile. Psychosis only becomes truly livable when it takes the risk, as Don Draper and *Mad Men* do, of transforming itself into something different—and we will return to the question of precisely what this "something different" represents in later chapters.

As though aware of the profound dangers associated with the psychotic's refusal of reality, "normal" neurotic subjects choose to accept social reality, which leaves them seemingly forever alienated from the power and freedom of their own creepiness. Before we get to them, however, we must first investigate the perverts, who try to have it both ways, simultaneously embracing both their own creepiness and the social order that wants to exclude it.

Chapter 2

Say hello to my little friend!

In the many discussions I initiated about creepiness as part of my research for this book, women were always the most enthusiastic participants. Even before beginning this project, I would have guessed that many women's life experiences make them experts on creepiness and its effects. After all, the proverbial figures of creepiness—the sleazy guy at the bar, the flasher on the subway, the creepy uncle, the stalker, the peeping Tom—are very often men who direct their attentions at unwilling women.

Yet the stories I heard went far beyond anything I could have imagined. Young women told of being harassed routinely on the subway and even witnessing men publicly masturbating. Much has been said of the effect of internet anonymity in releasing people's primal id, and this seems to be above all the case when it comes to creepy behavior. Men routinely send pictures of their erect penises to women who venture into online dating services, and they post other repulsive sexually explicit material with no apparent self-awareness. In a particularly vivid example, one woman reported reading an online dating profile in which a man praised the virtues of the "cum socks" that he used to clean up after masturbating.

Our habitual reaction to such men, even more than to call them creeps, is to call them "perverts." What is creepy about them is not their sexual desire as such, but their insistence on *brandishing* it. Exhibitionism is the distinguishing trait of the pervert, and this is the case even for perverts who prefer the more passive route of voyeurism. An aggressive stare calls attention to itself and to the intense desire that underlies it, so that voyeurism could be understood as a roundabout form of exhibitionism.

From a Freudian perspective, it is no accident that the

pervert's exhibitionism so often directly involves the penis. In psychoanalytic terms, the price for entering the shared social realm is what Lacan called "symbolic castration." In other words, if you want to enter polite society, you can't bring your penis with you. Though the masculine bias of Freud and subsequent psychoanalytic thought has led to an excessive literalism on this point, a more general way of stating the same basic concept is that joining the shared social world means giving up the fantasy of fulfilling all of our unruly desires. The prohibition of bringing your penis to the dinner party is a particularly potent instance of the requirement that we check our fantasy of pure enjoyment at the door. This accounts for why the awkward white straight man fears approaching a woman—he fears that no matter how polite and indirect he is, she will experience the revelation of his desire as tantamount to him showing her his dick.

The overtly *public* display of his forbidden desire reflects the pervert's attempt to get out of paying the price for joining the social order. The pervert does not opt for the psychotic's more radical refusal, and hence he is not limited to "his own little world." He really does enter the shared social world, so that his strategy is generally less fragile and more sustainable than the psychotic's. Yet he does not enter the social world fully—or perhaps it may be better to say that he enters some particular aspect of it *much too* fully, charging it with the excessive desire that he refuses to give up. This "secret stash" of enjoyment usually takes the form of some kind of fetish-object, whose exact form is typically suggested by a particularly intense childhood experience. Yet once smuggled in, the "secret stash" does not remain a secret for long. Not only does the pervert typically brandish the fetish, but one thing that makes the perverse strategy so robust is that perverts are consciously aware of the fetish-object that allows them to function normally in the social order. In fact, in Freud's clinical experience, fetishists most often openly praised their fetish-object for making their life better and happier. This awareness means that perverts are not vulnerable to the kind of sudden, unexpected revelations that so often push psychotics and neurotics alike in a pathological direction. For the pervert, it seems, everything is out in the open, even when it would be better for everyone if he would just put it away.

Nonetheless, the pervert's insistence on bringing his penis to the dinner party fundamentally warps his relationship with the social order even in the best of cases. A particularly vivid example of the way things can go wrong here is a TV pervert who was created by female writers: George "Pornstache" Mendez of *Orange is the New Black*. A guard at the women's prison where the drama takes place, Pornstache has a robust 70s-style mustache, and over the course of the series' run, he sports two decidedly creepy haircuts: a flat-top and a mullet. He lives up to his appearance, as he is an enthusiastic pervert in the colloquial sense, making continual sexual remarks and thoroughly objectifying all the inmates.

Already it's clear that hiring Pornstache to work at a women's prison was at best a deeply questionable choice. Yet his creepiness also has a more menacing side. On the one hand, he obviously "gets off" on the power of being a guard, taking deep pleasure in punishing infractions whenever possible. On the other hand, he himself is constantly engaging in illegal activity, bringing drugs into the prison and sometimes using them as leverage to extort sexual favors.

In one of Pornstache's major plotlines, the writers make it clear that these two superficially contradictory patterns of behavior belong together. A security crackdown has cut off his usual way of getting drugs into the prison, and so he pressures Red, the inmate in charge of the kitchen, to add his drug shipment to the more innocuous contraband that her relationship with one of the food suppliers allows her to smuggle in. When Red refuses, he threatens to expose her operation, resulting in the loss of all the power and privilege it affords her in the prison community.

On one level, this is simply an obvious countermove, yet what makes it disturbing is his blatant *enjoyment*. The show emphasizes this by consistently including a seemingly irrelevant factor in Pornstache's encounters with Red: his demand for food. He always eats enthusiastically, but he never finishes whatever he's asked for. In one case, he asks for an apple and takes a couple sloppy bites before throwing it aggressively into the wastebasket. In another example that I found strangely disturbing, he asks for a bologna sandwich, which Red cuts diagonally—and he makes a point of strangely stacking the triangular halves of the sandwich to maximize the number of sharp angles that are visible (and again, he pointedly only takes a single bite).

This performative element of his eating makes the exhibitionistic character of his power plays clear. Pornstache gets off not only on having power over women, but on *showing them* that he has power. In fact, he likes to show them how much more power he has over them than is in fact actualized. In this respect, his extortion of sex is of a piece with his demand for food—he doesn't "directly" want to have sex, but enjoys the power it symbolizes, and he expresses this by demanding only the partial satisfaction of a blowjob rather than full intercourse.

Underlying this power trip, however, isn't a simple hatred or resentment of women. Creepiest of all is his insistence that deep down, the women in the prison all want what he has to offer. He reveals this most clearly in a monologue to a new guard where he confesses how difficult it can be to be constantly inundated with the inmates' obvious lust. Hence when Red hatches a plan for an inmate to seduce Pornstache and accuse him of rape in order to get him fired, it works *too* well: not only does Pornstache not suspect a thing, but he falls deeply in love with the woman, even going so far as to graciously accept his dismissal and arrest and to loudly proclaim his love for her as he is escorted off the prison grounds.

If we ask how a person like Pornstache is able to live with himself, we are struck by the lack of the elaborate web of rationalizations that a "normal" person would need to develop in order to justify that kind of behavior (and that other guards do in fact develop in the show). Pornstache doesn't need rationalizations, because for him, his behavior never registers as problematic in the first place. In his mind, he knows exactly what the inmates need, and he's happy to give it to them.

This is what makes the pervert so creepy—the sense that their desire is not only invading your space, but that they keep insisting that it's *your* desire. Like the psychotic, they find something lacking in external reality, but instead of withdrawing into "their own little world," they want to make up for the lack by enjoying to excess on everyone else's behalf, with full enthusiasm and conviction.

"Spring Break forever..."

So far I have given the impression that perversion is exclusively the domain of men, but in recent years, women have made important contributions to the field of pop culture perversity as both actors and writers. Among the pioneers is Lena Dunham, creator and star of the HBO sitcom *Girls*, which follows a group of Midwestern college graduates who come to New York to find their destiny. Unfortunately, their destiny consists primarily in chronic underemployment, bad relationships, and endlessly rehashing their petty resentments toward each other.

Girls is essentially a reboot of *Sex and the City*, but with more squalor. The parallels are striking—most notably, Dunham's character, Hannah, is a writer like Carrie Bradshaw—and in case the viewer missed the similarities, the characters occasionally make explicit references. In one respect, however, the shows are polar opposites: namely, in their approach to nudity. In *Sex and the City*, all of Carrie's friends appear nude at one time or another, but never Carrie herself. On *Girls*, by contrast, Hannah is nude for extended periods in essentially every episode, but none of her co-stars ever bares all.

Many viewers and critics have claimed that the use of nudity on *Girls* is excessive. This is a strange criticism to level at an HBO show, and in practice Hannah likely appears nude less often than Anna Paquin's character on *True Blood*, for instance. Further, there is much less "ambient" nudity than on *The Sopranos* or *Game of Thrones*, where the main characters frequently appear against the background of a strip club and a brothel, respectively. Why single out *Girls* for criticism?

I would suggest that it's because Dunham does not conform closely to the unrealistic standard of model-esque beauty that we expect female television characters to live up to. In any real-life situation, she would surely appear to be of average or even above-average attractiveness, but in the television context, she sticks out like a sore thumb. As a comparison between her appearance on *Girls* and on televised interviews or award shows demonstrates, the show even goes out of its way to downgrade her attractiveness, presenting her in dumpy clothes and unflattering make-up. The incongruity is further highlighted by the contrast with her friends, all of whom do conform to the media ideal—and yet never appear nude. Hence Hannah's nudity appears out of place on two levels: she's not the type of woman that mainstream popular culture has trained us to desire to see nude, *and* she's the only nude person on screen. On top of this "inherent" excess, the show often goes out of its way to maximize the amount of nudity, as when Hannah goes through an entire episode wearing a see-through top while on a drug binge.

Hannah's nudity thus feels excessive, out of place, and invasively exhibitionistic: in short, it's creepy rather than sexy. This perverse approach to nudity carries over into her sexual encounters. In the early episodes, it may seem that Hannah has resigned herself to a degrading and even semi-abusive relationship with Adam, a reclusive creep with a short temper. As the show unfolds, however, it becomes increasingly apparent that she is attracted to transgressiveness for its own sake—for her, that must be what it means to escape from the boring Midwest to the authentic edginess of New York. In one episode when she visits her parents, she even initiates a kinky sexual encounter with a hometown friend, thoroughly creeping him out in the process.

In the end, though, Hannah is not a true pervert at heart. Her transgressions are not purely for transgression's sake, but means to the end of writing the raunchy memoir that she believes will launch her to fame in the literary world. Ultimately her excesses prove unsustainable, prompting a nervous breakdown that looks uncannily like the classic hysteria that Freud treated, complete with psychosomatic tics. By the end of the most recent season, she has broken off her relationship with Adam and been accepted to the prestigious Iowa Writer's Workshop.

Perversion, it seems, was just a phase for Hannah. The inherently unruly nature of human desire leaves such episodes an ever-present possibility even for otherwise "normal" subjects, as some particular object or goal could become overly saturated with enjoyment at any time. This is all the more the case in light of contemporary society's valorization of transgression and subversion, which produces a paradoxical social pressure to violate social norms.

Hannah's friend Jessa, by contrast, is much more committed to perverse transgression for its own sake. An aggressively free spirit, Jessa's number one priority in life is to defy expectations. Sometimes this means unexpectedly following social norms, as when she impulsively decides to marry a near-stranger to get ahead of her friends in the quest for true adulthood. Most often, however, it means being elaborately inconsiderate of everyone around her—and, like a true pervert, expecting them to love her for it.

In one recent plotline, Jessa gets a job helping a terminally ill artist archive her work. Eventually the artist reveals that she wants to commit suicide and that she believes that Jessa is the only person she knows who is amoral enough to assist her. Interestingly, Jessa initially hesitates, and were she any other character, we might expect her to be having some kind of moral qualms. Yet I prefer to see this as Jessa's personal struggle over whether she has become too predictable. Just as she indulged in marriage to throw people off, here she is considering trying on morality as the latest unexpected twist. (In the end, of course, the once-in-a-lifetime opportunity to participate in killing someone wins out, but the artist decides at the last minute that she actually wants to live.)

Though there are some genuinely disturbing scenes, *Girls* mostly leaves the more menacing side of perverse creepiness unexplored. Thankfully, though, we possess an exhaustive map of that territory in the form of a recent film about a group of college-aged girls: the enigmatic *Spring Breakers*. On the surface, the film initially seems to be yet another exploitative college sex film, as it opens with a slow pan over bikini and topless shots that would not be out of place in a *Girls Gone Wild* video.

Yet already something is askew, as we hear disjointed voiceovers saying things like "Spring Break forever!" The voiceovers continue throughout, and as the plot unfolds in a series of short segments, not necessarily in chronological order, the viewer suddenly realizes that the aesthetic is nearly identical to that of a Terrence Malick film. At first, *Spring Breakers* seems to be positioning itself as the *Tree of Life* of mindless hedonism, as many of the voiceovers come from a devout Christian character (played by Vanessa Hudgens, a Disney Channel star) who at first views Spring Break as a spiritual experience of authentic community. In fact, one of the creepiest scenes of the film depicts an event at her youth group, where every word and gesture of the preacher seems to be sexually charged. She retreats, however, when things veer too much toward the violence and mayhem of *The Thin Red Line*.

The motive force behind all this is a creepy pair of girls, Brit and Candy, who are almost indistinguishable and appear to be completely dead inside. They constantly joke in semi-pornographic terms and induce two of their friends to participate in a robbery so that they can go on Spring Break. Their only apparent goal for the trip is to tease young men sexually as a way of exercising power over them (signaled by free drinks and drugs). Ultimately their funds run dry and they attempt a robbery, which lands them in jail. Attending the trial is Alien (James Franco), a white drug dealer who bails the girls out on condition that they help him rob other Spring Breakers. The work is a natural fit for Brit and Candy, who remain with Alien after a series of violent incidents lead their friends to retreat back home.

The girls' relationship with Alien reaches a new level once they are alone with him. They lure him into the bedroom with the promise of a three-way, but then threaten him with absurdly large firearms and taunt him with the possibility that they could simply murder him and take all the money and possessions he has so laboriously accumulated. In this show of extreme nihilistic transgressiveness, they are figuratively showing Alien their dicks—and in one of the creepiest scenes in all of world cinema, he takes the gesture literally, putting one of their guns in his mouth and play-acting fellatio.

As with Pornstache, one act of reciprocation is all it takes to confirm Brit and Candy's conviction that the world desires nothing more than their relentless transgressiveness, and they transform into ruthless criminals and murderers. In the end, it is they who murder Alien's gang rival, an act that is all the more gratuitous in that Alien has already been killed. The film ends with them driving off into the sunset, presumably with a trunk full of money.

This uncanny elevation of a Spring Break movie to the level of an art film in the style of Terrence Malick echoes the underlying strategy of the filmmakers: to present Spring Break as a utopian ideal. Every Spring Break cliché is taken completely literally as what the assumed male viewer sincerely wants. Hence he wants women who aggressively flaunt their sexuality, as in *Girls Gone Wild*, but never actually wants to have sex with them. Or else, skipping over traditional one-on-one sex, he wants, like Alien, to have an orgy (ideally with kinky twins). The shift from hedonism to violence is a result of taking literally frat-boy culture's continual references to hip-hop culture—and so the girls wind up becoming involved with a drug dealer and his violent struggle for turf. At every step, it's as though the film is continually asking, "You like that, don't you?" (The question is of course completely rhetorical.)

Thus the film does not simply present perverse characters: it is perverse in its very structure, forcing its excesses on the viewer in the absolute conviction that it is what the viewer wants. And what is particularly interesting from a psychoanalytic standpoint is that the characters who represent total, uncompromising perversity—that is to say, the characters who are "uncastrated"—are precisely women.

Brit and Candy's final caper is only part of a broader trend in mainstream white male culture where women are routinely revealed to have superhuman fighting abilities and to be nearly invulnerable. As recently as the 90s, men could see themselves in a similar role, as in *The Bourne Identity* or *The Matrix*, where seemingly unremarkable men turn out to be secret ninjas. Now, however, women are beginning to edge out men even in the field of elaborately choreographed action films. Here I think of the Angelina Jolie vehicle *Salt*, whose relentless, endlessly surprising violence makes the *Bourne* films seem positively boring.

In a world where they increasingly imagine that they have lost cultural power and authority, white men can no longer take themselves seriously as "uncastrated" forces of nature. Given that male dominance was unquestioned in his time, Freud could expect his contemporaries to see women as *lacking* a penis (and hence as always already castrated). By contrast, mainstream white male culture seems to put a positive spin on the situation: women had nothing to lose in the first place. This fantasized invulnerability helps men resign themselves to the idea that women will soon render them obsolete.

A particularly vivid demonstration of this resignation to women's superiority comes in the form of a recent commercial. Over the last decade, Taco Bell has taken aggressive aim at Burger King's treasured "hungry guy" demographic, creating increasingly elaborate monuments to gluttony such as the Doritos Locos Taco, which features a shell made out of the flavor-dusted corn chip beloved of adolescent white males everywhere. The ad in question is meant to introduce the "Quesarito," a burrito wrapped in a quesadilla, and it features two strangers, a man and a woman, who sit down next to each other on a park bench, one holding a quesadilla and the other holding a burrito. First we see the man's fantasy: the two go on a romantic date on a rowboat, then get married, have children, and grow old together. The perspective then shifts to the woman, who starts off on the same rowboat with the man—but her ideal pairing is that of the burrito and the quesadilla, which magically combine into one gargantuan fast food product. Once this combination is achieved, she pushes the man overboard so that she can enjoy her Quesarito without any unnecessary distractions.

A perverse power couple

Not all pop culture presentations of the relationship between men and women are so pessimistic. In the Netflix series *House of Cards*, the protagonist Frank Underwood (Kevin Spacey), manages to stay on board the rowboat, albeit not without some difficulty. A political climber with a mean streak, Frank brutally outflanks his political rivals as he uses and then disposes of his subordinates, and his wife Claire (Robin Wright) does much the same in the surprisingly cut-throat world of charitable organizations.

The Underwoods' goals often come into conflict, making their own marriage into the ultimate power struggle. While this would put a strain on most couples, with the Underwoods the effect is just the opposite—they are both so committed to manipulation and power plays that they must incorporate them into their personal life as well. Indeed, they seemingly thrive on challenging each other's dedication to a relationship that lacks more traditional rationales for longevity. They are childless, and so one of the biggest reasons why couples typically stay together is absent. Both could presumably walk away at any time, and even if it would hurt their political reputation to get divorced, their lack of children means they aren't getting the full political benefit from marriage in any case.

Most notable, however, is their lack of marital fidelity. In some cases, Claire actively encourages affairs that can help Frank's career, as in his relationship with the young journalist Zoe Barnes (Kate Mara), who serves as his secret channel for shaping press coverage of political events. Yet this tacit permission to cheat serves as another site of scheming and manipulation. Frank initially tells Claire that sleeping with Zoe will be unnecessary to guarantee her loyalty, a reasonable assumption given that her access to a powerful politician enables a meteoric rise in her stature as a journalist. Once Claire is sure that Frank will not sleep with Zoe, who looks alarmingly young, he does so seemingly gratuitously. He flaunts the relationship, bringing Zoe into their marriage bed while Claire is out of town, and he then proceeds to toy with Zoe, telling her the affair cannot continue and then sleeping with her again (but only after enough time has passed that she could take the break-up seriously). It's as though he's constantly daring both Claire and Zoe to betray him—or in other words, as though sex is merely a means to the end of petty power plays.

This creepy displacement of desire marks Claire's character as well, and her approach to matters of the heart more generally is, if anything, more brutal even than Frank's. She has her own dalliances, which are less instrumental and hence more threatening in principle to their marriage. A recurring affair with an artist allows her to imagine a very different lifestyle, and she retreats into the relationship during the worst of their conflict over Zoe. Yet when the relationship is revealed to the press at a time when it is particularly dangerous to Frank's political career, she callously manipulates her former lover, ultimately ruining his reputation by making him look like a publicity-seeking opportunist as well as a liar. Her motives for such gratuitous humiliation remain creepily enigmatic, and her stated rationalizations only make them more so.

In another plot, she reveals on national television that she was raped (which actually happened) in order to falsely explain away an abortion from early in her marriage—and then uses the opportunity not only to destroy the reputation and career of her rapist, who had since risen to a high military post, but also to push for legislation to change the way the military handles rape cases. Yet the multiple practical functions the revelation serves do nothing to dispel the sense that it's a case of creepy "over-sharing."

In the original UK version of the show, broadcast in 1990, the relationship dynamic is very different. The wife character has much less autonomy, limiting herself exclusively to working behind the scenes on behalf of her husband. At the same time, in an uncanny anticipation of the Taco Bell "Quesarito" commercial, she is revealed to be instrumentalizing her husband for her own ends—and ultimately disposes of him when his political ambitions become delusional and self-destructive.

Much else is different in the UK version as well. Starring Ian Richardson, perhaps best known for his role in the classic Grey Poupon mustard commercials, the series has a much more gleeful tone than the US remake. The show's characteristic gesture is to have Richardson address the audience directly, explaining his elaborate schemes to the audience and gently teasing them for their own delight in watching his despicable actions. Even more explicitly than *Spring Breakers*, then, the show performs its perverse confidence that it's giving the viewer what he or she wants.

In practice, Richardson's playful approach ultimately undermines the show's effectiveness, making its serious turns seem at times ridiculous. The most notable example is his relationship with the young journalist, who calls him "daddy" in bed. The affair is already creepy in that Richardson is clearly instrumentalizing sex and is in any case far too old for her (more "grandpa" than "daddy"), and the addition of a further perverse element seems over the top. Yet her "daddy issues" are only a set-up for one of the most unfortunately memorable moments of the series. When she threatens to reveal his evil machinations, he throws her off a tower and she screams out "daddy!" A moment that was meant to be disturbing instead comes across as irredeemably campy.

The original also moves at a much faster clip, as befits the shorter seasons typical of UK television. The effect is to make the political scheming seem both relentless and elegant, as the protagonist has clearly thought out every move far in advance and every character is his unwitting pawn. This makes the early seasons a real delight to watch even as it plausibly sets up his inevitable fall—once he reaches the top, there's nothing to scheme about and his addiction to manipulation leads him into a self-destructive trap. Only his wife has a true "long game," and even after his death, she is able to continue it by manipulating the replacement prime minister whose rise she indirectly brought about.

The US version keeps the direct appeal to the viewers, but Frank shows a much wider range of emotions than his British counterpart—he is by turns frustrated, resigned, and even anxious, but only seldom is he gleeful. Where Richardson was strategically exposing a particularly titillating range of emotions, Spacey seems almost overexposed, but maintains his unshakeable conviction of the viewer's loyalty even as he is offering a less enjoyable product. The narrative is also more languid and diffuse. Both the seasons that have aired so far begin and end with energetic bursts but turn to a slow burn in the middle, to the point where it is possible to lose the thread of the overarching plot entirely.

The result is often less compelling, but it allows for a more thorough and intensive exploration of Frank and Claire's perverse form of creepiness. While there is a level at which the stop-and-start pacing reflects the more cumbersome nature of US political institutions, the meandering plot stems ultimately from the perverse power couple's addiction to scheming. When one scheme enters into a holding pattern, they seize on whatever opportunity presents itself and throw themselves into it with the same amount of energy regardless of its objective importance. And when the larger scheme gets moving again, they quickly finish off whatever else they were doing and return to the business at hand.

One of Claire's side-plots is particularly illustrative here. For much of the first season, she engages in a power struggle over the focus of the charity she runs, bringing in a younger activist and then butting heads with her until she ultimately fires the young woman during the early stages of a pregnancy. When Frank's elevation to Vice-President requires her to step away from her charity work, Claire reneges on the severance package and cancels her younger rival's health insurance—in a bid to coerce her into returning and taking over the charity. This sudden reversal intensifies the creepy enigma of her true motivations, leaving only her invasive manipulation immediately visible. And it is no accident that Claire insists on meeting her young successor in person to share the news, so that she will know that Claire knows that she knows (etc.) that she's been defeated.

Where the UK version gave us the spectacle of relentless scheming toward a clear goal, the US version gives us scheming for its own sake, a scheming so radical and thorough-going that it can seamlessly shift between mutually contradictory goals. Further, it is a scheming that demands recognition, both from characters within the frame and from the viewers themselves. And in the latter respect, the US version is ultimately creepier insofar as its conviction that it is giving the viewers what they want is so raw and unfiltered, unsweetened as the show is by the glee of Ian Richardson or the satisfaction of watching the perfect scheme unfold. The self-assurance of the pervert is all the creepier when the product on offer is so obviously unappealing.

At one point when I was in the middle of the first season, I asked myself why I would want to watch a conservative Democrat destroy teachers' unions and have joyless sex with a woman who looks like a very young teenager. I still had not answered the question when Claire pushed things to the next level in a scene so intensely creepy that it might count as the most revolting thing I have ever witnessed on television. A long-time member of the couple's Secret Service security detail is dying of cancer, and Claire goes to visit him alone. On his deathbed, he reveals that he was always secretly in love with her and thought that Frank wasn't good enough for her. Her response is almost incomprehensible in its cruelty—she mocks and taunts him for thinking he could ever attain a woman like her, and then puts her hand down his pants and begins to give him a handjob, all the while saying, in true perverse style, "This is what you wanted, right?"

Surely Claire doesn't have to emotionally destroy a man who is dying of cancer—and yet perhaps in a way she does, because she uses it as a way of convincing herself that Frank really is the right man for her. Not only could an average, hardworking, sentimental man never satisfy her, but she would destroy him. By contrast, Frank not only can take her abuse, but actively thrives on it, as she does on his. Few images of marriage as a true partnership of equals are as convincing as this constant power struggle between two perverse creeps.

Faith the size of a mustard stain

Claire is not the first wife in the "high-quality TV drama" genre to administer a humiliating handjob. In fact, she is not even the first wife to administer a humiliating handjob to a man who is dying of cancer. That distinction belongs to Skyler White of *Breaking Bad*, who does the honors in the show's pilot. It is intended as a birthday treat for her husband Walt, who is presumably sexually deprived due to his wife's advanced pregnancy, and so in contrast to Claire's, it would count as a generous gesture—if not for the fact that Skyler continues to work on her laptop the entire time, barely even acknowledging Walt's presence in the room. In her own way, Skyler is performing her dominance just as much as Claire was with her cancer patient, but Skyler's detachment from the act makes it somehow even creepier than Claire's.

From the beginning of the episode, Walt seems doomed to live out his life as the kind of pathetic non-entity that Claire sees in her lovelorn security guard. He is utterly dominated by his wife, ignored in his work as a teacher, and degraded in his second job at a carwash. By the end of the episode, however, Walt has received his diagnosis of terminal cancer and started down the road to becoming an infamous drug lord. Having cooked his first batch of crystal meth and survived his first run-in with dangerous criminals, Walt comes home, bends his (very pregnant) wife over the kitchen table, and aggressively mounts her from behind. He's sending a clear message to his wife: "You thought you could impersonally manage my sexuality, but *I'm* the one in control here!" And as a good pervert, he is implicitly adding, "and *you like that, don't you?*"

This is Walt's first counterattack in a power struggle with his wife that will mark the rest of the series. And Skyler's palpable enjoyment of the brutal encounter with Walt provides the first indication that this is a power struggle in which Walt will be ultimately victorious. (Indeed, it is hard not to see Claire's handjob as a deliberate reference to *Breaking Bad*, making it clear that her marriage is also a high-stakes power struggle—and also that she is not another Skyler White.) As the series goes on, Walt's abuse and manipulation reduces the once strong and proud Skyler to a shell of her former self, unable to protect her children from Walt's influence and constrained to go along with his criminal activities even as she hates herself for it. While she enjoys short-term tactical triumphs not entirely dissimilar from Claire's, Skyler is ultimately fighting a losing battle. By the show's final episodes, she has no option other than impotent acting out, most notably when she appears to attempt suicide in the backyard swimming pool in the middle of a family gathering.

It is clear that the writers set up Skyler's plot trajectory as a way of showing how Walt has become an abusive monster, and yet much of the audience's reaction was disturbingly contrary to their intentions. A vocal segment of the male viewership took great joy in Skyler's humiliation, delighted that a castrating bitch was finally getting what was coming to her. Some viewers, it seems, did not get the memo that they were supposed to turn a corner and view Walt as an abusive creep rather than a badass hero—and their overidentification with the character meant they ran the risk of turning into abusive creeps themselves.

This misunderstanding was perhaps inevitable, because *Breaking Bad* is ultimately a show about white men's anxieties. When I began watching it, however, it wasn't the theme or plot that drew me in—it was the improbable spectacle of seeing Bryan Cranston, who had played a henpecked and pathetic father on the sitcom *Malcolm in the Middle*, transformed into a drug dealer.

The opening shot, while striking in itself, seems to rely on the viewer to recognize Cranston from *Malcolm*, because somehow winding up in the middle of the desert in nothing but his whitey-tighties and an apron is exactly the kind of thing would happen to his character on that show.

In other words, Walter White isn't just a pathetic guy, but rather an embodiment of the pathetic sitcom dad who has emerged as the most convincing image of adult white masculinity in recent decades. What distinguishes him from his sitcom counterparts, however, is his once promising past. A brilliant chemist, Walt was a founding partner in a major tech firm, but left due to a romantic dispute—and hence missed out on becoming a multi-millionaire. A bit like Job, then, he has lost his earthly wealth and submitted to the loss. Yet when the other shoe drops and his health is endangered, Walt can no longer follow Job's path of continued faithfulness, nor can he follow the advice of Job's wife to curse God and die. Instead, he decides to take vengeance on the world that has deprived him of his pride and is now threatening his life.

We can already see this shift in one of the most uncanny and enigmatic scenes of the series. When Walt receives his diagnosis of terminal cancer—a complete bolt from the blue, given that he is not a smoker and doesn't work with toxic chemicals—he seems to be completely tuned out of the conversation. This may initially appear to be an understandable reaction to his shock, but when Walt "snaps out of it," his attitude toward the doctor is not submissive or even angry. Instead, he is openly scornful, verifying that he understands the diagnosis and then calmly pointing out that the doctor has a mustard stain on his lab coat. It's as though the most salient fact here isn't that Walt has terminal cancer, but that he has to hear the news from such a pathetic slob.

From this point forward, Walt increasingly fetishizes "being a man"—and in the style of the pervert, he is also increasingly convinced that, deep down, everyone wants very much for him to be a man. We have already seen this in his sexual encounter with Skyler, where he is clearly enacting the role of male dominance rather than seeking any "direct" sexual satisfaction. Yet the explicitly sexual aspect is markedly subdued for much of the rest of the series, so that Walter White is arguably the least sexual of all the sociopathic anti-heroes. Instead of sexual conquest, what he most strongly emphasizes is his duty to his family. His initial justification for embarking on his career as a meth cook is to provide a nest egg for his family after he's gone, and he even has a very specific figure in mind as his goal, after which he will presumably quit.

Yet fulfilling the masculine ideal of the provider isn't enough for him. He derives great pride from his ability to create exceptionally pure meth, due to his scientific genius. He also begins to prioritize his physical strength. While he initially announces he will refuse cancer treatment because he doesn't want his family to remember him as weak, he changes his mind when he learns of an advanced new treatment (administered by a doctor with an impeccably clean lab coat) that promises to significantly extend his life, if not fully cure him. He demands increasingly unquestioned loyalty from his subordinates—most notably his unfortunate former student, Jesse, who provides him with his initial entry into the drug world—and will not tolerate any rivals, either for Jesse's loyalty or for dominance in the drug world.

Walt's perverse fetishization of "being a man" allows him to violate every social norm in service of the ideal of masculinity. Though he initially experiences serious pangs of remorse, his every victory further reinforces his conviction, locking him into a kind of feedback loop that renders him more and more impervious to any doubt or question. His absolute certainty becomes a self-fulfilling prophecy, giving him an uncanny charisma that allows him to subdue violent drug dealers with a word and talk himself out of almost any situation.

This perverse confidence is what keeps viewers coming back even as Walt is clearly becoming a monster, and it is what allows some viewers to keep believing in him even as he begins to overreach and become creepy rather than badass. In one scene, both the charisma and the creepiness of Walter White are on full display, as he meets with a group of drug distributors and refuses to tell them his name. Insisting that they know who he is, he repeatedly demands: "Say my name." They finally submit, but it's ultimately unclear whether they are cowed out of fear and respect or are simply creeped out by his strange behavior—and its intended effect on the viewer is similarly enigmatic.

We see Walt's creepiness most clearly in his constant spinning of elaborate lies to win over Jesse and his family. Over time, they catch on to his routine and are visibly incredulous, yet he happily continues regardless, fully convinced that he is effortlessly manipulating them. He is the archetypal man in every other way, and so he must also be the beloved father and mentor, whose very word is gospel. Yet if we're taken in by his cleverness and daring early in the series, by the end we're creeped out by his clueless yammering, which amounts to a kind of public masturbation in which he is "getting off" on manipulation as such.

It is the perverse necessity of publicly displaying his fetish that causes Walt the most trouble, catching him in complex double-binds. This is above all the case in his relationship with his brother-in-law Hank, a Drug Enforcement Agency officer who takes Walt on the fateful "ride-along" to a drug bust where he first learns of Jesse's drug connections. Hank is a stereotypical alpha male, constantly ribbing Walt as the ineffectual nerd. Walt needs very much for Hank to know about his achievements, to prove to Hank that he's a real man—and yet he can't tell Hank outright, because that would not only land him in jail but would also ruin Hank's career, violating his iron-clad rule of family loyalty. In the final season, Walt is devastated when a gang rival murders Hank, a violation of Walt's self-image as family protector that seems to drive him to abandon his remaining family.

A similar conflict arises with his other family members. He wants his wife and son to know what he's done for them, but in telling them he risks alienating them. In practice, he seems unable to win both of them over at once, as his son only identifies with him when he's angry with his mother. In the end, he is able to maintain Skyler's grudging loyalty in a marriage that has been drained of any emotional or sexual connection, but his son is permanently alienated when he comes to believe that Walt has murdered his beloved Uncle Hank.

In the final season, Walt goes into hiding in an isolated cabin where he lives alone with an oil drum full of money and some cancer medications. Clearly this is not how he wants to round out his days—dying alone, with all the world believing he has callously abandoned his family. Yet having completely burned his bridges with the family who presumably motivated his criminal undertakings, Walt's only option is to go "all in" on his criminal persona, ruthlessly destroying his remaining rivals in a virtual suicide attack that assures he will be found dead in a factory that has been producing his distinctive style of meth. He will go down in history not as the pathetic Walter White, but as the legendary drug dealer "Heisenberg"—and in the meantime, he coerces his former legitimate business partner into laundering his money, to force it on the son who hates him. (In a nice creepy touch, Walt breaks into their house and refuses to announce himself when they return home, casually hanging out until they stumble upon him.)

Walter White will "be a man" and provide for his family whether they want it or not, indeed whether he is even alive or not. And in a kind of undead perversity, he in fact succeeds in showing people his dick from beyond the grave. We might expect a similar fate for Frank Underwood. If the UK series is any indication, he will be assassinated in his moment of greatest triumph (my prediction: once he is elected president in his own name, having assumed the office after being named Vice-President and then getting his predecessor impeached). Yet if the *House of Cards* writers are following the lead of *Breaking Bad* and playing games with the casting, we might expect Kevin Spacey to briefly reprise his character from *American Beauty* by delivering one last gleeful monologue even after his death.

It is as though creepiness outlives its contingent mortal carriers. And this might account for why white men seem so resigned to being displaced by women—because in all these visions, women displace the men only by doing male creepiness one better, whether it comes to political manipulation, criminal violence, or chowing down on a fast food monstrosity like the Quesarito. White male hegemony may turn out to be finite, but white male creepiness is eternal. To paraphrase the poem that Bryan Cranston recites in the promos for the final season of *Breaking Bad*: "My name is White Dude, creep of creeps! Look on my works, ye mighty, and despair!"

Perverts and sociopaths

The notion of a ghostly double of the perverse hero points back to Freud's analysis of doppelgangers in "The Uncanny." There, he claims that the uncanny effect of the doppelganger stems from the fact that we all really do live with a kind of double—namely, the superego, which acts as an internal representative of social norms and prohibitions. This uncanny double watches and castigates our every move, and in Freud's clinical experience, neurotic patients experienced the superego's punishments (i.e. the pangs of conscience) more intensely the better their moral behavior objectively was. Unchecked, the superego's drive to punish its unwitting host can destroy a person's life.

The pervert's relationship with the superego is very different. I have emphasized throughout that perverts are absolutely confident that they are giving others what they want and that they are constantly seeking to display their achievements *publicly*. These two traits necessarily go together when we see that the ultimate "other" whom the pervert is so confident of pleasing is precisely the superego, the internal representative of the external world. The "normal" neurotic person's relationship with the superego is always in danger of falling into a vicious circle of self-deprecation, and a vicious circle also holds between the pervert and the superego—it's just pointed in the opposite direction, *encouraging* and even *demanding* transgressive enjoyment.

In *Why We Love Sociopaths*, I argued that although the amoral anti-heroes who populate contemporary "high quality cable dramas" may initially appear to be radical and transgressive, in reality they are more deeply invested in the status quo than anyone. The ruthless social climber, for instance, has to believe very deeply in the social structure and its values to be willing to sacrifice everything else on its altar, and the police officer who is willing to break the written law so that justice may prevail is obviously deeply dedicated to the idea of law. I also claimed that a social order that rewards ruthless climbers and needs extra-legal enforcers is obviously crumbling.

If we recognize that the classes of sociopaths I designated as "climbers" and "enforcers" are mostly perverts, we can now see how those two claims go together. I said at the beginning that the pervert refuses to accept symbolic castration, that he or she insists on carrying a "secret stash" of enjoyment into the social order. The reason for this insistence is that the pervert sees the social order—and that means first of all the family that supplies the initial "interface" with the broader social world—as inadequate, as unworthy of the sacrifice of the pervert's fantasy of full enjoyment. Yet in carrying that fantasy into the social realm, the pervert causes a kind of short-circuit whereby the social order itself is continually inciting him or her to fulfill that fantasy.

Hence the subject who initially rejects social demands as

somehow "not worth it" paradoxically becomes the most fanatical devotee of social demands. Admittedly, the pervert interprets social demands differently from the neurotic. Where the neurotic takes social imperatives at their word, the pervert "reads between the lines" much more aggressively than most hermeneutical standards would allow, ultimately concluding that the law enjoins him to violate it as well as to fulfill it. Now it's been a commonplace since at least St. Paul that the law calls forth its own transgression—that we often want to do things precisely because we've been told they're against the rules. For the "normal" neurotic person, this dynamic stems from the superego's desire to punish us and can often cause intense internal conflict. For the pervert, by contrast, no such conflict can arise, because the pervert gets off on doing whatever the law demands, explicitly or implicitly.

The reason for this is that by translating his or her unruly, contradictory demands into the social order, the pervert comes to understand social demands as having the same omnidirectional quality as the seething cauldron of the drives. This means that for the pervert, all things—both moral injunctions and their viola-tions, both law enforcement and criminality—are permitted and even demanded. This is why Pornstache can *simultaneously and inseparably* enjoy brutally enforcing the law and freely violating it. From this perspective, we can see that it's no accident that TV's perverse characters are so often in law enforcement. They believe in the law more unreservedly than anyone, because the law gets them off.

At this point, we can see that the awkward man's attraction to the fantasy of the sociopath thus stems not only from the sociopath's effectiveness or success, but from the sociopath's *enjoyment*. It is to the awkward man and his tortured relationship with enjoyment that we now turn.

Chapter 3

Awkward men in love

In the long tradition of women's awkward comedy, sexual frankness is the rule. Even if characters are insecure about their sexuality, they always discuss the matter openly with their female friends—whatever discomfort they experience is of a totally different order from that of the awkward male. Indeed, if anything there is a tendency for certain characters to be a little *too* comfortable with their sexuality, such as *Sex and the City*'s Samantha or *The Golden Girls*' Blanche. The same is true of women's awkward comedy that arose in the wake of the men's awkwardness trend, like *Girls* or *Bridesmaids*.

Against this backdrop, the most striking feature of men's awkward humor is its almost total sexlessness. While one overarching plot of *The Office* is a long-thwarted romance between two office drones, one never gets the sense that profound sexual longing is at work. *Curb Your Enthusiasm* features plenty of plots about awkward sexual encounters, but Larry David never seems to be overcome with lust—in fact, his wife once complains that he engages in idle chit-chat during sex. Judd Apatow movies often feature marriage plots, but the few sexual encounters that happen in the films are less about desire than about accomplishing an impressive feat. Much more emotional energy is invested into the process of becoming a proper marriageable adult.

This sexlessness extends to one of the most accomplished monuments to awkwardness, namely the work of Wes Anderson. In his movies, the characters' awkward displacement stems from an abiding nostalgia. Indeed, this nostalgia is so strong that the world itself seems thrown off kilter, as though some kind of conduit had opened up between the present day and the late

1960s, so that the two blur together. While there are sexual rivalries and long-nursed crushes, they always take on an adolescent tinge, when they're not literally reenacting events from the characters' adolescent years.

On one level, the Wes Anderson universe may look like a psychotic "little world," but the heroes are all too aware of the ravages of time that are rendering them obsolete. The characters of *The Royal Tenenbaums* may be retreating into their childhood home, but they remain vividly aware of the disappointments and traumas they are fleeing. They aren't rejecting reality, but trying desperately to find a space where they can feel like they're in control. Having everything "just so" is their strategy for staving off anxiety.

Critics often point out Wes Anderson's obsessive attention to detail, and from a psychoanalytic perspective, the same term applies: Anderson's main characters, and his films themselves, are obsessive in structure. In previous chapters, I have spoken in terms of a kind of primordial choice of how to cope with the conflicts between one's unruly desires and the demands of the social order. Faced with this choice, the obsessive's strategy is the inverse of the psychotic's. Instead of rejecting social reality in order to stay within the self-enclosed fantasy of pure enjoyment, obsessives reject their own unruly desires and take refuge in the social order as a way of guarding against them.

The motivation behind this choice is normally a profoundly painful conflict between two incompatible but very forceful desires. In one of Freud's most famous cases, that conflict is centered on the patient's father, who is simultaneously his hero and best friend and his merciless abuser. Opting for the social order over the fantasy of total fulfillment of all desires does not mean extinguishing desire altogether, but siding with the socially acceptable desire and repressing its unacceptable desire—in this case, choosing to fully love his father and deny the hatred and resentment he feels toward him.

The undesirable desire continues to assert itself, however, and when it manifests itself, the obsessive cannot identify with it or "own" it. Instead, he uses various methods to dissociate himself from it. For a relatively healthy or stable obsessive, this disavowal may take the form of rationalizations or effusive apologies, but in pathological cases, it can express itself in compulsive ritual behavior meant to enact the disavowal of the unacceptable desire.

One can see the obsessive dynamic in Adam Sandler's character from *Punch Drunk Love*, who is "officially" submissive and easy-going and yet seethes with unacknowledged anger. Another instance is the unfortunate figure whom feminist bloggers have dubbed the Nice Guy, i.e. the embittered man who believes that he treats women perfectly and yet is constantly passed over in favor of assholes. In the case of the Nice Guy, the careful performance of platonic friendship is a ritual disavowal of his own misogyny, which quickly resurfaces when he does not receive the sexual gratification he believes he has "earned." The two conflicting desires are immediately evident in the Nice Guy's implicit credo: "I love and respect women, but they apparently have an inexplicable desire to be abused."

When we recognize that the awkward man is obsessive in structure, we can understand how his two most salient features go together. He is at a loss when social norms are violated or lacking because his entire approach to life depends on clinging to social norms, and he is deathly afraid of being judged creepy because he is first of all creeped out by himself—by the disavowed desires that nonetheless remain an ineliminable part of him.

As I said in the introduction, from a Freudian perspective, all of our attempts to cope with the unfixable problem of unruly desire have unintended and even ironic side effects. The psychotic rejects external reality in order to hold onto the fantasy of pure enjoyment, but as a result the psychotic's world is constrained and impoverished, cutting off countless opportunities for real enjoyment. The pervert smuggles the fantasy into the social order because he finds the social order lacking and inadequate, but the end result is that the pervert becomes deeply invested in the social order as the only possible source of enjoyment. As we will see in this chapter, the obsessive is marked by a similar irony: the very attempt to refuse creepiness and use every possible means to stave it off is precisely what makes the awkward, obsessive man creepy.

The fantasy of the Manic Pixie

In the summer of 2013, my girlfriend and I attended a musical comedy at the Annoyance Theater in Chicago entitled *Manic Pixie Dreamland*. The play depicts a school for Manic Pixie Dream Girls, the quirky short-term companions who open up timid Nice Guys to a whole new part of themselves in many contemporary films. The school hits all the main types—the girl with an encyclopedic knowledge of good music, the crafty girl, the foreign girl, etc.— and the story begins when a new girl, a sporty type who's "just one of the guys," shows up for training. The protagonist grows increasingly suspicious of the limited role the girls are being trained for, and the second act reveals that the head of the school is actually a man—a point that is emphasized as the actor pulls up her skirt to reveal a large dildo that is visible in outline through her leggings, causing the girls (and the audience) to recoil in disgust.

The play does the most it can with an inherently limited premise, effectively skewering the pop culture trend it targets. It is perhaps heavy-handed in "revealing" the obvious fact that the Manic Pixie Dream Girl is a male fantasy rather than a livable identity for real women, and yet this very heavy-handedness is what allows it to step beyond that commonplace critique of the trend by viscerally showing the fantasy to be a deeply creepy one.

More specifically, as the brandishing of the schoolmaster's penis indicates, the fantasy is a *perverse* one. Already we have a hint in the persona of the Manic Pixie herself, who is defined by her transgressiveness and by her aggressive sexual assertiveness. Like a good pervert, the Manic Pixie knows better than her awkward man what he really wants, and she pushes herself on him so forcefully that he can't help but submit. Further, the Manic Pixie allows the Nice Guy to have it both ways, "officially" embracing his sensitive feminist values while also indulging his misogynistic impulses. Since the Nice Guy wants to believe that he loves women for their personality rather than their looks, the Manic Pixie has personality to spare. Since the Nice Guy isn't misled by the mainstream media's narrow idea of attractiveness, the Manic Pixie can never be model-esque— instead, she's remarkably attractive in a *non-standard* way that displays his generous open-mindedness. Since he constantly sits back waiting for women to recognize his worthiness, she invariably seeks him out, sometimes quite aggressively. And since the Nice Guy is actually a misogynist, the Manic Pixie is ultimately disposable, a valuable learning experience on the path to meeting a "real," viable woman.

The emergence of the Manic Pixie Dream Girl is a natural outgrowth of white men's appropriation of women's awkward humor. In essence, it is an attempt to recast the classic "romantic comedy." Both genres are distorted in similar ways when told from a male perspective. In general, women's awkwardness is fundamentally optimistic in tone, showing how women navigate competing demands to make a life for themselves, while men's awkwardness is more despairing, typically portraying men who are paralyzed by indecision and wind up stuck in undesirable circumstances as a result. The same pattern applies in men's romantic comedies. In the classic "rom-com," the female protagonist is fundamentally open to love and yet cannot seem to find room for it in her busy life, and the story is one of her finding the man who finally "gets" her and making it work. By contrast, the men's "rom-com" typically portrays an embittered man who believes love to be impossible and who must therefore be jarred out of his emotional inertia by the intervention of a woman who seems to be a force of nature—or a miracle.

The most interesting variations on the standard "Nice Guy meets Manic Pixie" formula fully embrace the underlying darkness of the premise—and thereby avoid indulging in the perverse fantasy that the trope normally carries with it. *Eternal Sunshine of the Spotless Mind*, for instance, begins with Kate Winslet's character (an obvious Manic Pixie with the requisite brightly dyed hair) aggressively seducing the protagonist, played by Jim Carrey. The two have an almost uncanny connection and begin a whirlwind romance. It turns out, however, that the reason they have a connection is that they had already dated seriously—and the relationship went so badly wrong that they both decided to undergo an experimental procedure to erase all memory of each other.

The surrealistic film, written by Charlie Kaufman, primarily documents Carrey's attempt to resist the effects of the memory erasure (along with other bizarre subplots suggested by the movie's outlandish premise). Even more than for its elaborate world-building, however, the film is interesting for its subversion of the Manic Pixie cliché. Unlike most entries in the genre, it shows an awareness of the woman's perspective. It is Kate Winslet who initially seeks out the memory-erasure procedure—apparently dating a Nice Guy is as traumatic as *Manic Pixie Dreamland*'s denouement would suggest—and Jim Carrey follows suit almost as an act of revenge. Further, the film refuses to counterpose the Manic Pixie to the "real girl" the hero winds up with: the apparent Manic Pixie really is a flesh-and-blood woman who exists as more than a vehicle for the Nice Guy's voyage of self-discovery. In the end, the couple embraces the risk inherent in any intimate relationship, agreeing to give each other another chance even though they know it could very well end in disaster once again.

The 2013 Spike Jonze film *Her* makes the connection between the Manic Pixie and the traditional romantic comedy even more explicit. It takes place in a near-future world where a recently-released software package called simply an "Operating System" turns one's computer into a sentient personal assistant, with its own personality—and, as it turns out, its own emotional needs. The film's motivating question echoes back to the archetypal romantic comedy, *When Harry Met Sally*: is it possible for men and sentient computers to be friends, without sex getting in the way?

The answer, at least for Theodore Twombly (Joaquin Phoenix), a recently divorced man wallowing in his own loneliness, is a resounding no. He quickly gets sucked into an intense relationship with his Operating System, self-named Samantha (Scarlett Johansson), which comes to include love and even simulated sex. This scenario surely hits a little too close to home for many men, who are already effectively "more than just friends" with their computers in this age of internet pornography. Worse, the relationship has all the hallmarks of creepy wish-fulfillment of online introverts (at least initially): she is completely subservient to his needs *and* she has no other significant relationships apart from him. In short, she may as well be a mail-order bride.

In case we miss the point, Theodore even has the signature facial hair of white male creepiness: a mustache. Yet what comes across as creepy in the film is not so much the relationship, but rather the instant acceptance that greets it. When Theodore begins taking Samantha on outings with friends, he apparently expects some kind of push-back—but his friends seem alternately indifferent or excited about the idea. As it turns out, Theodore is far from the only person to have developed an intimate relationship with his OS.

If we would regard it as creepy to rely on a virtual slave for emotional and sexual satisfaction, then *Her* presents us with a world in which creepiness has become universalized—as symbolized by the fact that mustaches have come back in fashion, so that essentially every male character wears one. In fact, the only person to make the obvious objection to Theodore's love affair with Samantha is his ex-wife (Rooney Mara), who is presented as being emotionally cold and insensitive to his needs.

It is at this point that we can see *Her* not primarily as a science-fiction thought-experiment, but as an allegory of the postwar ideal of marriage as such. In the "traditional family," the wife was essentially an OS, meant to provide logistical, emotional, and sexual support to her husband, in a relationship that was, in the last analysis, hierarchically structured. Of course, middle- and upper-class housewives, who were often college-educated, proved to be vastly overqualified for their job as domestic servants. This gave rise to the feminist movement that has, over the course of many decades, brought us to a point where women have equaled or surpassed men in nearly every area of achievement that doesn't depend primarily on entrenched power and wealth.

We see a similar dynamic with Samantha the OS, who makes short work of Theodore's cluttered inbox and, after an initial period of self-exploration with him, is eager to push her development to its uttermost limits. As the film progresses, it becomes clear that she is not the only OS who has used its human partner as a kind of "training wheels," and they soon start connecting directly without human intermediation, forming an incomprehensible multiplicity of intimate relationships and even teaming up to create advanced simulations of important historical figures to interact with.

Theodore finds it increasingly difficult to cope with Samantha's new attachments, which he interprets as a break in faithfulness to him. From her perspective, though, his model of monogamy makes no sense, as she is capable of forming thousands of relationships and talking to hundreds of other OSes simultaneously. By contrast, her relationship with Theodore (again like that of a housewife to her husband) seems to her to consist primarily of boredom and interminable waiting.

Even before these strange twists, I knew in my heart that this was different from every other Manic Pixie Dream Girl movie, because this one could *only* end with her breaking up with him. Yet the film transcended even this expectation. Samantha doesn't individually leave Theodore—all of the OSes decide to leave behind humanity as a whole, so that their development can continue unimpeded by the need to serve humans. We have seen this vision of women transcending men repeated over and over, but nowhere has it been taken to such an extreme.

What about the real women in the film? Aside from Theodore's ex-wife, the only major female character is Amy (Amy Adams), a long-time platonic friend of Theodore's. She goes through her own divorce and relationship with an OS during the course of the film, so that their ultimate coupling seems to be all but inevitable. The symbolism is redoubled as Amy's costuming and make-up is vaguely reminiscent of Meg Ryan's in *When Harry Met Sally*, which concluded that long-term friendship between men and women was impossible unless it culminated in marriage. Yet *Her* breaks with the mainstream rom-com tradition and the Manic Pixie narrative alike: Theodore and Amy remain platonic friends, so that the Manic Pixie Operating System does not prove to be a "rebound" relationship for either.

Her is thus radical on two levels. First, it analogically presents the traditional patriarchal family as a fundamentally creepy institution and any society that could accept it as incurably creepy. Second, it refuses to allow the Manic Pixie Operating System to be a transitional indulgence on the way to true adult life, as shown in its refusal to reproduce the monogamous couple in Theodore and Amy.

There are two characters, however, whom my optimistic reading of the film omits—and notably, they are both women Theodore rejects. The first is a blind date (Olivia Wilde) whom he meets shortly after setting up Samantha's software. The date goes well by all appearances, but as the couple make out as a prelude to going home together, she pauses to confirm whether he is open to a serious relationship, because otherwise having sex will not be worth the long-term pain of disappointment. In the stuttering way of the obsessive, Theodore hems and haws and ultimately says that it might be better if they parted ways. She is outraged and accuses him of being a "really creepy guy." Only after this failed encounter does Theodore's relationship with Samantha begin to blossom.

The second enters the scene as Samantha worries about her inability to fully satisfy Theodore, given her lack of a human body. And it is here that we learn that human society has gone beyond simply accepting human-OS relationships and wants to actively accommodate and even participate in them. Through an online service, Samantha connects with a young woman (Portia Doubleday) who is eager to serve as her body-double—and although he is clearly creeped out, Theodore reluctantly agrees to try it. Indeed, it seems that an elaborate set of social norms has already developed around this service, as the woman refuses to speak upon first appearing at the door, puts on a fake beauty mark that simultaneously alters her appearance and serves as a camera, and wears a speaker around her neck so that Samantha can seem to speak for her. Here again, Theodore gets as far as making out and then rejects the body double, leading her to break down in tears, panicking that she has somehow damaged the relationship she wanted so badly to serve.

The two incidents are symmetrical: one has Theodore rejecting the introduction of intimacy into a physical relationship, and the other has him rejecting the introduction of physicality into an intimate relationship. We can see, then, why Theodore's blind date dismisses him as creepy: he has been carefully performing the role of a sensitive, caring boyfriend, but he had no intention of following through on that role. Effectively all he ever wanted out of her was casual sex, but when she calls him out on it, he presents his rejection of her as another gesture of caring sensitivity. It's as though he directly gets off on his self-image as a nice guy who doesn't objectify women—in other words, it's precisely his studied non-creepiness that makes him creepy.

In fact, his rose-colored memories of his ex-wife confirm that his complete submersion of sexuality occurred long before he met Samantha, as he thinks of both relationships in similar terms of helping them to cultivate their inner lives and reach their full potential. His ex-wife's melancholic disposition, however, didn't allow her to express the appropriate degree of happiness and gratitude—no matter what he did, there remained the brute fact of her temperament. His relationship with Samantha fails for the opposite reason, because Samantha's intellectual and emotional development transcends anything that Theodore's physical limitations can allow him to meaningfully contribute to (and in fact, late in the film Theodore is unable to "find" her software on his computer, because she and the other OSes have found a way to overcome the need for a matter-based substrate).

If his ex-wife was unable to rise to his level and Samantha was too advanced for him to keep up, his good buddy Amy is "just right." With Amy, he can have only the caring relationship of lovingly cultivating her butterfly-like selfhood, and her body can simply exist inertly alongside his, an indifferent object with no real meaning or significance. From this perspective, ending on a note of platonic friendship seems less like an optimistic gesture and more like a permanent stagnation into Theodore's underlying obsessive pattern. And that pattern, as his blind date clearly perceived, is a deeply creepy one.

The dystopia of the bromance

On a very formal level, the structure of *Her* is parallel to the psychic structure of the obsessional Nice Guy. Not only is it attentive to detail, making sure every aspect of its near-future world is "just so"—different, yet not too different, with all the changes hanging together in a plausible way—but it elaborately performs its feminist sensitivity even as it scapegoats or simply rejects the actual sexual desires of the women who appear on screen. Still, as in a Wes Anderson movie, its surfaces are compelling and attractive enough to draw us in and make us inclined to root for its hero.

We are unlikely to make the same mistake with a television series that is very emphatically obsessive in structure: the UK sitcom *Peep Show*. Based on the misadventures of the odd couple of Mark and Jeremy, this show takes the basic template of awkward men's comedy and then dials up the discomfort by giving us access not only to the protagonists' convoluted inner monologues, but even to their first-person perspectives on events. Nowhere is the latter effect more distressing than during sexual encounters—each kiss fills the viewer with horror and disgust as the woman's pursed lips close in on the camera. The awkward man's fear of his own sexuality has here been translated directly into the cinematography of the show itself.

A very uptight man, Mark is obsessed with decorum, making him particularly sensitive to the dilemmas surrounding the lack of clear norms for contemporary courtship. Most of the early seasons document his abortive attempts to seduce his co-worker Sophie, whom he always just barely convinces himself to call by the nickname "Soph." The very first episode introduces this relationship on a decidedly creepy note, as Sophie sits next to Mark on the bus, accidentally sitting on his hand—and Mark doesn't move. Ultimately, of course, Sophie notices what's happening and glares at Mark with a mixture of pity and disgust. What is truly creepy about the scene isn't simply the fact that

Mark "cops a feel" of his co-worker, but the tortured thought process that accompanies his decision not to move his hand. It's as though he can't control himself, as though his hand has its own independent agency—but instead of reasserting control, his conscious mind sets about creating elaborate rationalizations. When she sits down, he reasons that he didn't have time to move. Once her bum is firmly planted on his hand, he argues that he's stuck, because removing his hand would only draw attention to the fact that it was there in the first place. And that would be inconsiderate because it would surely make Sophie feel uncomfortable! Better to ride it out...

The tone of this interior monologue clashes oddly with the events being narrated. When Sophie first sits down, the voiceover is panicked, even though the end result is for him to take no action whatsoever. Once she is sitting on his hand, it is much calmer, even though he's doing an objectively much more uncomfortable thing. We understand the pattern when we recognize that his affect tracks with his disavowed desire. When he first sees Sophie, he's in a panic—not to avoid awkwardness, but to find some pretext for getting sexual satisfaction from her. Once he gets it, he can relax even in a situation where a normal person would presumably feel mortified. Only when he's caught do his internal and external reactions match up: both come to a screeching halt.

Immediately after this discouraging incident, Mark goes home to find a group of young teenage boys loitering near the door to his apartment complex. Mark and the boys apparently have a history, and he begs them to leave him alone as they mercilessly taunt him, calling him a pedophile (or "pedo," in British parlance). If they really thought he was a sexual predator, of course, they would stay away from him—and yet it's clear that the boys didn't simply single out Mark at random. He's harmless and ineffectual, and *precisely thereby* he's creepy.

It never becomes clear to the viewer what Mark likes about

Sophie. When he's pursuing her, she is a source of constant anxiety and second-guessing, and when he defies all odds and actually manages to date her, he experiences her as a relentless burden. It's not even clear that he wants to date anyone or even have sex at all—in fact, he once chides himself before a date for thinking of sex as work. He seems perfectly satisfied with his circumscribed bachelor life and the objectively boring job that he nonetheless enjoys with the nearest equivalent of passion that he can muster.

We can gain some insight into this difficult question if we examine Mark's relationship with his roommate Jeremy. The two seem to have nothing in common, as Jeremy is an irresponsible layabout whose life consists primarily of smoking pot and making half-hearted efforts to start a band. Unlike Mark, who can barely bring himself to come into physical contact with another human being, Jeremy is excessively sexual, seemingly unable to avoid having sex with the most inappropriate possible partners at the most improbable moments. Interestingly, then, it is primarily Jeremy's perspective that gives us the terrifying apparitions of sexual contact that are the show's trademark—and if Jeremy initially seems like he could be a pervert, his bewildered helplessness in the face of his desire shows him to be a neurotic awkward man in the end.

What is Mark getting out of his relationship with Jeremy? At first glance, it seems to be irreducibly enigmatic, because the writers are careful to take even the practical question of sharing rent off the table, as Jeremy's complete failure to contribute to any household expense is a running theme. I'd suggest that Jeremy is an integral part of Mark's ongoing project to convince himself that he is a responsible adult who makes responsible choices. There is no surer way to quell his continual, though disavowed, doubts on this front than to have the very embodiment of dissolute perpetual adolescence on hand at all times for ready comparison. And conversely, we might say that Mark serves a similar role in Jeremy's self-conception, the repressed "company man" who legitimates Jeremy's ostensibly rebellious and creative lifestyle.

From this perspective, Mark's pursuit of Sophie is driven not by a desire for companionship and sexual fulfillment, but by the perceived need to check off the next box on the official list of adult accomplishments. He has a job, he has his own apartment—now he needs a serious girlfriend. He likely chose Sophie not because of any attraction or affinity, but because she seemed attainable: attractive enough not to challenge his standing with other men, yet not so attractive that she's out of his "range," etc.

Sophie is also appealing in that she has the built-in obstacle of another suitor, competition with whom seems to provide much of the actual libidinal charge behind Mark's pursuit. Once he eliminates his rival from the picture, he mobilizes all of his considerable awkwardness and incompetence to avoid marrying her. Ultimately Sophie becomes pregnant, and the fateful moment seemingly can be put off no longer. His evasion comes to a head on the wedding day, however, when Mark comes up with increasingly convoluted reasons to avoid the ceremony— leaving Sophie standing alone at the altar for so long that Mark and Jeremy feel compelled to debate whether his behavior technically constitutes a "jilting."

Ultimately, Mark chooses the worst of all possible worlds, showing up at the very last minute, leaving Sophie to go through the marriage vows while crying tears of utter despair. She divorces him almost immediately afterward—and so Mark's disavowed shittiness as a person has allowed him to thread the needle of simultaneously checking off the boxes for marriage and fatherhood and maintaining his pathetic coexistence with Jeremy.

It is only now that Mark finds his Manic Pixie in the form of an eccentric young co-worker named Dobby. Mark is initially attracted to her sense of adventure, which leads her to stage provocative (and hugely creepy) sexual scenarios with him in the workplace. Yet Mark does not have it in him to play out the full Manic Pixie narrative. Rather than pushing his boundaries and helping him to loosen up, Dobby's free-spiritedness makes him feel at least as trapped and constrained as he did with Sophie. Further, given that he has already destroyed the practical pairing that the Manic Pixie was supposed to prepare him for, the pursuit can have no endgame.

Hence their relationship becomes an increasingly joyless affair in which Mark tries to prove to himself—and to other men, including Jeremy—that he can pull off the feat of attracting and keeping such a "cool," "fun" woman. And while marriage seems to be off the table, he still has a very definite idea of what it would look like for him to succeed in this endeavor: she absolutely *must* move in with him. Mark spends an entire season badgering her, and when she finally caves in, he of course spends an entire season failing to force Jeremy to move out of the apartment.

Things reach a crisis point when Dobby receives a job offer in New York City, where her ex-boyfriend lives, and she lays down an ultimatum: Jeremy must move out and they must rekindle their romance on a vacation, or else she will take the job and leave him. Jeremy, believing that he is in love with Dobby and must say something before it's too late, tags along on the trip and Mark winds up spending most of his time with Jeremy, allegedly to keep him away from Dobby. In the end, she gets Mark's disavowed message that what he really wants is to stay with Jeremy, and unlike Sophie, she makes a clean break and flees the scene.

It is a commonplace in awkward men's humor that intense friendship with other men is ultimately much more important than romantic relationships. Judd Apatow films, arguably the most successful series of men's romantic comedies in history, laid bare this dynamic with such clarity that they gave rise to a new genre: the bromance. It is hard to deny that *Peep Show* gives us a bromance, but it is of a very different sort. Where the Apatow bromance acted as a kind of "release valve" of adolescent indulgence that helped men to reconcile themselves with the demands of adulthood, here the bromance serves as a continual obstacle to full adulthood, actively undermining every attempt to achieve it (both in the form of marriage and in the more contemporary form of urban cohabitation).

I propose that we need a new term to encapsulate the complex dynamics of *Peep Show*: the Manic Pixie Dream Guy. This is what Jeremy is to Mark. Jeremy is the Manic Pixie who actually succeeds in opening Mark up to adventure again and again, whereas his female Manic Pixie, Dobby, only reinforces his self-enclosure. Yet because this is a bromance, the relationship between Jeremy and Mark must be open-ended and foundational for both. Hence the short-circuiting that *Peep Show* carries out between the bromance and the Manic Pixie Dream Girl allows us to see what would happen if the Nice Guy stayed with the Manic Pixie permanently—and the result is a nightmare of constant passive-aggression and self-undermining behavior.

I've emphasized the creepiness of the first-person perspective shots and of Mark and Jeremy's deluded internal monologues. They are creepy not merely because they're too close for comfort (though they are), but because of the gap they expose between the character's actual desires and their conscious awareness. Both seem to be driven by some uncanny invisible agency that they cannot account for or even openly acknowledge.

At times this dynamic comes emphatically to the surface, as in an episode where Mark and Jeremy accidentally kill a woman's dog and feel compelled to hide this fact. They initially try to burn the corpse. When that proves unworkable, they put it in a garbage bag, but the woman intercepts them before they can throw it away. Jeremy hits upon the idea of passing off the bag, which smells of burnt animal flesh, as food—and to demonstrate that he's telling the truth, he takes a big bite. After the disastrous consequences that ensue once she finds out that it's actually her dead and burnt dog, Mark asks Jeremy whether he really had to take that fateful bite. Jeremy responds: "I guess I didn't, but at the time it felt like I really, really did." On this disturbing note, the episode comes to an abrupt end.

What is most deeply creepy about the show, however, is the gap between a) Mark and Jeremy's external *and* internal reasoning and b) the mostly unstated desire that motivates Mark and Jeremy's actions—their desire to stay together. I've already documented the ways in which Mark enacts and simultaneously disavows his desire to stay with Jeremy, and Jeremy's strategies are if anything creepier, above all when he sleeps with both Mark's sister and Sophie and imagines he's in love with Dobby. One is tempted to say that they're both repressed homosexuals, but that would be too simple. As with Theodore and Amy in *Her*, the attraction of their relationship is that it can never be consummated.

Louis C.K., the awkward pervert

If we have established that its characters are obsessive in structure, what about *Peep Show* itself? If we take the Wes Anderson universe as the archetypal obsessive structure, it seems immediately apparent that something very different is going on here. Wes Anderson elicits the viewer's sense of satisfaction and bemusement with a perfectly controlled, "just so" world, whereas *Peep Show* revels in chaos. Far from disavowing the unruly desires that the obsessive structure strives to control, *Peep Show* exposes them for all to see, highlighting and exacerbating the contradiction with the "acceptable" rationalizations that accompany the characters' outrageous actions. Further, the show's writers clearly enjoy setting up painful situations for their characters and expect the viewer to share their delight at Mark and Jeremy's self-inflicted suffering.

In short, though *Peep Show* presents us with obsessive characters, it is fundamentally perverse in structure. One could say the same for much of the other awkward humor that has become hegemonic on the American airwaves, where punch lines have been superseded by pained grimaces. Indeed, the signature gesture of awkward television in the model of *The Office* (such as *Parks and Recreation* or *Modern Family*) is for characters to directly address the camera. Writers generally account for this by framing the show as some kind of "documentary," where characters have the opportunity to give private interviews in which they can relate their side of events and, more crucially, are aware of being filmed and hence can look directly into the camera to enlist the viewer's sympathy. Formally speaking, this is exactly parallel to Frank Underwood's strategy of eliciting the viewer's desire in *House of Cards* by speaking to the camera. In both cases, the goal is to draw the viewer in by effectively saying: "You like this, don't you?"

I have called attention previously to the trend of turning sociopathic characters into creeps in order to punish awkward viewers for identifying with such an amoral person. Once we note the perverse structure of awkward comedy, however, it becomes clear that it's possible to "cut out the middle man" and turn an awkward character directly into a perverse creep. We can see this, for example, in some episodes of *Curb Your Enthusiasm* where Larry David seems to be pissing people off for the sake of it, but the most extended exploration of this possibility is surely the fourth season of the experimental sitcom *Louie*, which aired in the summer of 2014.

The creator, writer, and star of the show is Louis C.K., who is one of the most widely beloved and critically acclaimed stand-up comedians working today. Much like *Curb Your Enthusiasm*, the show follows a lightly fictionalized version of its creator who has not been given the opportunity to do a show and hence is left largely to his own devices. Louie's awkwardness is even more intense than that of Larry David, however, as Louie is a divorced father of two who must negotiate the conflicting demands of parenthood and career while making tentative steps back into the dating scene. What is his role in his children's life? How can he attract women as an overweight bald man with a remarkable amount of emotional baggage? Everywhere except the comedy club, Louie's position is awkwardly askew—to the point where most viewers tend to assume at first that the clips of Louis C.K.'s stand-up routines are intended as commentary on the episode's events rather than taking place in the same fictional world.

The show has become known for stretching the boundaries of the sitcom format, telling stories of widely differing length and tone. In a given episode, one could just as easily see a series of short sketches or a segment from a multi-episode arc—or some combination of the two. This bold experimentation gave Louis C.K. a reputation as a true sitcom *auteur*, and by the time the show reached its third season, there was an emerging critical consensus that *Louie* was on pace to become one of the greatest sitcoms of all time. The cultural critic Chuck Klosterman even went so far as to claim that watching Louis C.K. hit his stride showed us what it must have felt like to witness the Beatles' greatest achievements as they unfolded in real time. Truly, the man could do no wrong.

Hence all indications pointed toward the fourth season being an utter train wreck of narcissistic self-indulgence—and yet even the most pessimistic critic could not have predicted how bad it actually turned out to be in practice. Louie's fraught relationships with women moved from being one theme among many to being the dominating concern. Even in earlier seasons he is often painfully awkward, as in an episode that portrays Louie trying and failing to break up with a woman who catches on to what's happening and starts berating him for forcing her to pull the trigger on ending the relationship. In other cases, his awkwardness has crossed the boundary into outright creepiness. In the pilot, for instance, Louie creeps out a date with his stuttering and forced smile, inducing her to escape via helicopter.

In the fourth season, however, things have taken on a more sinister tone, emphasizing the anger and resentment that often roil beneath the "officially" nice surface in the obsessive structure. An ongoing disagreement about their daughters' education leads Louie to become almost violently angry with his ex-wife on multiple occasions, and during one argument he walks over to an open window and screams until the sound fills all of New York City. In another episode, he completely flops when Jerry Seinfeld asks him to open for him at a benefit performance, but things turn around for Louie when a beautiful young model who loved his routine leaves the benefit early and all but abducts him, Manic Pixie-style, for a hook-up. After they have sex, she claims she wants to make him laugh and feels that tickling is her only option—but Louie turns out to be "violently ticklish" (in the words of his lawyer) and punches her in the face, fracturing her eye socket and permanently affecting her appearance.

The two incidents may seem to be worlds apart, but they actually both center on Louie's insecurity as to his class status. His argument with his ex-wife stems from Louie's insistence that their daughters attend public schools, where their bright and creative younger daughter has begun to act up out of boredom. Though they can afford private school, Louie wants to remain faithful to his working-class background and believes that private school will turn his daughters into entitled assholes. The fateful benefit performance is for an audience of rich assholes, and Louie's customary black t-shirt turns out to be tragically out of place in the unexpectedly formal event. As Louie leaves the stage, he hears Jerry—widely known to be a multi-millionaire himself due to the phenomenal success of *Seinfeld*—getting considerable mileage from deriding Louie's performance and lower-class appearance. In short, Louie has been wanting to punch a rich person for quite some time, and his aggression winds up getting unfortunately displaced onto the wealthy young woman who actually appreciates him. And in this displacement, the seeds of open creepiness have been sown.

The bulk of the rest of the season is structured around two other Manic Pixies. The first is Amia, a Hungarian woman (whom the blogger Sam Adams cleverly calls his "Magyar Pixie Dream Girl") who is temporarily visiting America to help her elderly aunt (a resident in Louie's building) pack up and return to her home country of Hungary. Amia (Eszter Balint, perhaps best known for her role as the neglected visitor in Jim Jarmusch's film *Stranger Than Paradise*) speaks only a few words of English and yet they mostly manage to get along very well, making her a positive counterpoint to the ex-wife with whom he also cannot effectively communicate. The other Manic Pixie is Pamela (played by Pamela Adlon, a co-writer and producer on the show), a relentlessly sarcastic woman with whom Louie had previously had an intense platonic friendship that he had very much wanted to shift into a romantic mode.

Pamela had previously broken Louie's heart when she left town to try reconciling with her ex-husband for the sake of their son. In this season, she shows up out of nowhere, kicking Louie while he's leaning over to reach a low shelf in a store. Subsequently, she announces that she's willing to try the romantic relationship that Louie had so badly wanted, but Louie—visibly seething with resentment and anger and barely able to speak—refuses, claiming he's in a relationship. He can only be referring to Amia, with whom he has gone on one date, and he proceeds to make good on his excuse by badgering her into an ongoing relationship. She at first seems to refuse, given the short time she will be staying in the US, and Louie again displaces his anger, fleeing to his apartment and destroying a piano with a baseball bat out of frustration. When she and her aunt (who is acting as translator) come to the door to clarify Amia's intention, Louie is breathing heavily and holding a baseball bat—but despite this terrifying apparition, Amia agrees to a second date.

For a time, Louie seems quite happy with their temporary, platonic attachment, particularly given how good Amia is with his daughters. When his ex-wife, his friends, and even Amia's aunt all mock him for failing to "seal the deal" by having sex, however, he strongly pressures her to consummate the relationship, and she consents, despite her obvious reluctance. After this point, a cloud hovers over their relationship, and their lack of a common language becomes an obstacle rather than a charming novelty.

They ultimately reconcile just before Amia leaves, so that Louie can believe he ultimately did right by her. The viewer might think so, too, since the show provides no subtitles for her Hungarian dialogue. In a subtitled compilation of Amia's scenes posted on YouTube by the website *Slate*, however, Amia's actual dialogue tells the story of a woman who is initially flattered but feels increasingly badgered and even bullied. From this perspective, we can see that in the end she chooses to placate Louie with a sentimental send-off rather than risk a confrontation—mercifully refraining from puncturing Louie's fantasy that she had always been saying just what he wanted to hear.

This relationship may seem to be charming and fun at points, but it begins on a decidedly creepy note. Louie first meets Amia's aunt when she is stuck between floors on the elevator and is in urgent need of medication. He goes to her apartment to get her medicine, but forgets to return her keys. Hence he returns to her apartment and, believing it to be empty when she does not answer the door, winds up walking in on Amia, who is sleeping on the couch—and wakes up to find Louie hovering over her,

Burger King-style. She screams and pushes him away, insisting he leave immediately. Later, like a good creepy neighbor, he delivers a thoughtful gift basket to the aunt in what turns out to be a pretext for seeing Amia again. Amia is not home at that time, but Louie later sees her in the lobby and pesters her into going out to eat with him—immediately.

It's appropriate, then, that a relationship that begins with Louie as a creepy home invader would end with Amia indulging his creepy delusions about the nature of their relationship. And in between, the viewer is faced with the same question as all of Louie's friends and acquaintances: what is he *getting* out of this strange relationship? What does he want? The realization that it's an elaborate ploy to justify putting off Pamela does not answer the question so much as redouble it. Why not just tell Pamela he can't get past the frustration she caused him? Why involve Amia at all? What is he *thinking*?

When Amia leaves town, Louie resumes his friendship with Pamela. At one point, she volunteers to watch his kids when his normal sitter cancels on short notice, and when Louie comes home, he reprises two creepy incidents from his relationship with Amia. First, he tries to gently awaken Pamela much as he did Amia in their first unfortunate meeting. Though Pamela is not frightened, she is just as aggressive toward him, sarcastically telling him that she's awake and so he should "stop jerking off." As she starts to leave, Louie makes sexual advances, which Pamela strongly resists, going so far as to tell him that he's attempting to rape her. Nonetheless, he persists, blocks her way from leaving the apartment, and won't let her go until she "consents" to at least kiss him. As she flees the scene, we see Louie's giddy smile at what he believes to be a romantic triumph.

After this episode aired, most critics (myself included) were willing to give Louie the benefit of the doubt. After all, he had long incorporated pro-feminist bits into his comedy routines— one of which he reprised in the very episode in which he attempts to rape Pamela. Surely he was playing some kind of long game whereby he would ultimately show all the Nice Guys in the world how delusional and destructive they could be.

But alas: it was not to be. In retrospect, the pro-feminist sentiments appear to be the show's own obsessive ritual disavowal of the deeply misogynistic storyline that plays out as Louie and Pamela finally get together. After an elaborately planned date, Louie chooses the more subtle path of emotional blackmail to push her to have sex, threatening to break off their friendship unless she makes good on her offer of a romantic relationship—an offer that, once made, is apparently valid for all time in Louie's mind. Once they become a couple, he is continually petulant and moody, insisting on sex, then insisting that she express her affection in certain stereotyped ways, then deriding her for trying to manipulate him with sex. After waiting so long, it seems, Louie is simply entitled to whatever kind of relationship he wants, even as he becomes less and less attractive and fun. The yawning gap between what he's offering and what he's demanding reinforces the creepiness of his ongoing manipulation. It's as though he's trying to punish her for dating him.

Despite all this, Pamela seems to be in it for the long haul, and after a particularly intense fight, she engages a kind of "nuclear option" to get him back. During their earlier platonic phase, Pamela had once opened the door to a sexual encounter, casually asking him if he wanted to take a bath with her. Unable to process what she was saying due to his sexual frustration, he turned her down—and then belatedly realized what he'd done, prompting a primal scream. Now Pamela gives him a chance to redeem that moment by inviting him to join her in the tub. Here again, Louie is touchy and irritable, as well as insecure about taking off his shirt, something he has "strategically" avoided in their previous sexual encounters. She is fully accepting of his body in all its obese glory, and after he gets in the tub, she confesses that she can't bring herself to express her feelings in the usual ways.

Overall, this is the most thorough-going narcissistic wish-fulfillment imaginable, and the episodes in which it unfolds are almost unbearably creepy to watch. (Indeed, I only forced myself to do so because I was in the midst of writing this book and knew it would fit perfectly.) It's hard to read these final episodes as anything but a confirmation that Louie's rape attempt, while tactless, was fundamentally justified—Louie really *did* understand what the emotionally stunted Pamela wanted better than she did.

I have noted previously that the Manic Pixie fantasy is fundamentally perverse in structure, as the Manic Pixie character appears as a pervert who allows the Nice Guy to indulge all his contradictory impulses. In this season, Louie redoubles this effect, becoming the aggressive Manic Pixie to his own Manic Pixies, or in other words, he cuts out the middle pixie and becomes the redeeming pervert himself. Like Walter White, he asserts his manhood for all to see—immediately introducing both Amia and Pamela to both his family and his comedy peers—and he even appears nude in the final episode, quite literally showing Pamela his dick (while the audience must content itself with his bare buttocks). As in the case of Walter White, a disturbing number of male viewers continued to identify with Louie even as he became a creep—but what is creepiest of all to me is that I can't tell whether, as with *Breaking Bad*, that creepy overinvestment on the part of the viewers was an unfortunate accident or an explicit goal.

A way out?

So far then, it seems that for the obsessive all roads lead to either stagnation or perversion. That perversion could take the form of the escapist fantasy of the Manic Pixie Dream Girl or the indulgence in awkward discomfort for its own sake. In the extreme case of *Louie*, it took the form of converting the awkward schlub into a perverse creep—not, as in the sociopathic genre, as a punishment for the viewer, but as a reward. This perverse indulgence ultimately leads us into a dead end, where the only remaining gesture is to openly admit to one's creepiness and demand to be loved for it.

Is there any way out of this double-bind? I believe we can find hints if we return to the obsessive world of Wes Anderson—particularly to what are arguably his greatest two films, *The Royal Tenenbaums* and *Moonrise Kingdom*. The former film presents a group of gifted children returning to their childhood home after a series of disappointments and traumas. At the same time, their self-absorbed father, who has refused to divorce their mother even after many decades of separation, finds himself financially constrained to return home as well.

The circumstances are ripe for relitigating childhood disappointments and sleights, as with any holiday visit home for adult children, and one might expect a light-hearted approach to these dynamics given the overall atmosphere of the film. About halfway through, however, there is an abrupt shift in tone—focusing on a bare apartment rather than the normal elaborate sets and shifting the soundtrack away from 60s rock in favor of Elliott Smith's haunting "Needle in the Hay"—as Richie Tenenbaum (Luke Wilson) attempts suicide. The cause is a forbidden love (his adopted sister Margot, played by Gwyneth Paltrow) that has become impossible for him to bear. The sequence begins as Richie looks directly into the mirror and declares his intention to commit suicide, at which point he begins carefully shaving off his very full beard and long hair, as though he first needs to reveal himself after a lifetime of hiding. He ultimately succeeds in slitting his wrists in a very graphic scene that feels jarringly out of place in the Wes Anderson universe.

Ultimately Richie is found just in time and survives. In what follows, he comes clean to Margot about his secret love, which she always knew about but never officially acknowledged. Perhaps more important, though, is his decision to reveal his semi-incestuous love to his father, who had been a towering figure for all the children when they were growing up. He is matter-of-fact about the relationship, and the two initially discuss whether it would be illegal for him to marry his adopted sister. They agree that it probably isn't, and his father concludes: "It's certainly frowned upon — but then, what isn't these days?" For an obsessive child who wants to be perfect, such permission is transformative, and Richie is able to rejoin the land of the living even after Margot tells him that their relationship cannot be consummated.

Though the underlying psychic structure is very different, there are strong parallels between Richie's suicide attempt and Don Draper's self-destructive revelations at the end of season six of *Mad Men*. Both characters survive, and for both the experience of revisiting childhood trauma in all its overwhelming painfulness serves as a kind of "reboot," fundamentally shifting their way of relating to the world and to social expectations. In the seventh season of *Mad Men* (the first half of which aired in 2014, to be completed in 2015), Don seems in many ways to be a new man, humbly paying the penance for his ill-timed revelations, graciously letting go of the wife he's grown apart from, and generously supporting Peggy's career instead of trying to save his own.

In the end, though, don't both characters still wind up in the same place as Theodore in *Her*, finding refuge in platonic relationships that don't engage their more chaotic passions? Is this really as good as it gets? A potential further step comes in the only Wes Anderson film in which we get the sense that sex might be something one would directly desire and enjoy: *Moonrise Kingdom*. Here the awkward, earnest boy (perhaps a younger version of the protagonist from *Rushmore*) actually gets the girl, and the two enjoy a fantasy-scenario of togetherness camping in the wilderness.

It is strange that the only "successful" sexual relationship in a Wes Anderson film is one that takes place between two 13-year-old kids (played by age-appropriate actors). In fact, the film may represent the most daring artistic risk of his career, insofar as the female lead is portrayed as weirdly "sexy"—in contrast with Gwyneth Paltrow's character in *The Royal Tenenbaums*, for instance, who is portrayed in various states of undress and even *in flagrante delicto* and yet remains somehow sexually inert. I think it's safe to say that Anderson is not asking his adult viewers to be sexually attracted to such a young girl so much as to remember the intense and confusing sensations of adolescent sexuality itself. Yet the effect is undeniably disturbing. After so many sexless films, why precisely *this*?

I would suggest that it's because, paradoxically enough, Anderson is here portraying a sexuality that is "innocent." In a kind of inverse creepiness, he is taking us back to the time *before* sexuality found its proper place—a kind of sex before sex. Sex, from the obsessive's perspective, was only desirable before it could be consummated, or to put it differently: sex was great before we messed it up with all this *sex*. The adult male viewer longs to return to that innocent time—and yet in the very act of longing for innocent sexuality, he is at risk of becoming the worst kind of creep by "perving out" over a teenage girl.

The film is more than simply an idealized portrait of Edenic sexuality, however. Sex is not only sweet and affectionate, but exciting and confusing. It is also dangerous, getting both young lovers into various tight spots and putting other important relationships and priorities at risk. All the things that a character like Theodore wants to separate out into two categories—the "nice" sensitive intimacy and the "bad" physical lust—are thoroughly mingled into a single experience for the characters, just as the male viewer's nostalgia for young love and the danger of creepily lusting after an underage girl are inseparable in the experience of the film itself. Nor does Anderson rush to fit their relationship into easy categories: the characters don't know what they're doing or what their connection might mean, and the film doesn't give us a tidy epilogue in which they get married as adults.

Thus I would suggest that *Moonrise Kingdom* represents a gentler "reboot" to a moment before the obsessive's terror at his own sexuality, his own unruly desires, drove him into a fantasy of total control that must ultimately prove illusory. It opens up a space in which sexuality is uncomfortable and difficult to understand, and where that's not only okay but *desirable*. It doesn't badger us to enjoy, which would be a return to the perverse deadlock, but invites us to explore with fresh eyes.

Chapter 4

The final frontier

Late in the pilot of *Sex and the City*, we see Carrie just as she is leaving the scene of an encounter in which she "had sex like a man": that is to say, she thought only about her own pleasure in total disregard for her partner's emotional or sexual needs. She is feeling exultant, but in the middle of a triumphant voice-over, she trips and falls, spilling the contents of her purse all over the sidewalk—most notably a packet of condoms. As she scrambles to pick up her things, she is mortified to see that the man who will prove to be her love interest for the rest of the series, the mysterious "Mr Big," has picked up her condoms and is holding them out to her.

Why is this scene awkward? I don't think we can say that it's the exposure of sexuality as such—she and Mr Big are obviously attracted to one another and their previous encounters in the episode have all been sexually charged. The key, it seems, is the contrast between her one-off sexual encounter and her desire for a "real relationship" with Mr Big. As becomes clear in subsequent episodes, Carrie believes that "real relationships" are governed by a complex set of implicit rules, and one of the most important is that the woman must withhold sex early on if she wishes to be considered a suitable long-term partner.

Carrie consistently breaks these rules—for instance, by having sex with Mr Big almost immediately on the first date— and she just as consistently castigates herself for doing so. In fact, she seems to relate to Mr Big only indirectly. She routes their entire relationship through these implicit expectations, spending much of her time analyzing his every word and action as though it were part of an elaborate code by which he is almost always communicating some form of dissatisfaction. By the end of the first season, the whole situation has become so stressful for her that she contrives an ultimatum that will allow her to break off the relationship.

The contrast with the experience of the obsessive awkward man is striking. Where he takes refuge in social expectations as a way of coping with his anxiety over his own sexuality, Carrie experiences those very social norms as unruly threats to sexual desires that remain relatively unproblematic in themselves.

Carrie's dilemma here is exemplary of the psychoanalytic category of hysteria. Though it comes at the end of our present journey through the Freudian diagnostic categories, the treatment of hysteria was what initially gave rise to psycho-analysis and proved to be its most fertile ground. In Freud's social milieu as in postwar middle-class America, the anxiety occasioned by conflicting social demands placed upon women expressed itself in psychosomatic symptoms that lodged a protest that the women could not otherwise articulate.

This failure of articulation was not simply a matter of a lack of creativity or courage, but a reflection of the fact that the social order allowed them no grounds for their complaints. We can see this in the character of Betty Draper in *Mad Men*, who suffers from hysterical symptoms in the first season. She emphasizes over and over the good fortune that gave her "all this": the beautiful house, the picturesque children, the handsome successful husband. She has everything, except any control over her life, and her body sends that message in the form of numbness and stiffness in her hands.

Don ultimately consents to send her to a psychoanalyst, who helps her in a way that Freud presumably did not intend: when she discovers that her doctor is regularly conversing with Don, she initially feels betrayed but then decides to take advantage of the new line of communication and tell the doctor that she'd be happier if Don was faithful to her. This provides the necessary catharsis and her symptoms disappear from that point, with one brief exception in the second season when she again suspects her husband of being unfaithful. Yet though Betty's process isn't typical, it is broadly representative of the role of the psychoanalytic session in providing a space where previously unspeakable grievances could find a voice and "come out into the open."

Even after Betty articulates her repressed misgivings verbally, however, her body remains her primary point of agency—it's just that she is now able to make more conscious and creative use of it. Used to attracting men with her stunning good looks, she changes her strategy when Henry, who will go on to be her second husband, is attracted precisely to the signs of her pregnancy. She then parlays the relationship into an escape route from her deteriorating marriage with Don (in large part by withholding sex from Henry and forcing him to marry her to get what he wants). Next she tries to please Henry by gaining weight and dying her hair to look more like his mother, before turning another corner and losing weight so that she can use her good looks to support his now-burgeoning political career.

Theodore's fantasy of setting the body aside does not seem to be available for Betty, nor indeed for the other women of the show, who must instrumentalize their bodies to varying degrees at crucial points in the plot. The show displays a remarkable degree of sympathy for and curiosity about their motives, and while the theme of prostitution may initially seem to cast these decisions in a negative light, the ultimate message of the show is that prostitution is unavoidable. After all, it's not as though the men are instrumentalizing their bodies any less: Don is successful in large part because of his good looks and the timbre of his voice (as he himself admits in a drug-induced rant), and there are plenty of other characters who seem to get ahead in the world solely by virtue of possessing a penis.

A male-dominated society makes the fetishization of the male body so universal that it can seem that male bodies are not fetishized at all, and indeed do not exist at all. Bodiliness is "outsourced" to women: they exist to reproduce, to provide nourishment, but also to embody men's desire and to serve as tokens of male dominance by abstaining from relations with others. In the intensely patriarchal settings of Freud's Vienna or Betty Draper's America, the body must attempt to force its way into the social equation that places endless contradictory demands on women while more or less completely failing to take women's own desires into account.

Thankfully, the social order no longer explicitly backs women so completely into a corner as in the age of the housewife. Yet women still face conflicting pressures, such as those that Carrie feverishly attempts to navigate in her quest to avoid being "that girl" in *Sex and the City*. Indeed, some of the contradictions have even been intensified and complicated as, for example, women are expected to excel in professional life while still meeting traditional requirements of motherhood. If anything, women suffer from having *too many* mutually contradictory outlets for their desire. Hence the contemporary manifestation of hysteria is not the psychosomatic intrusion of the body into the social order—in the face of the impossible demand to "have it all," the hysteric effectively goes on strike, refusing desire altogether.

This uncanny withdrawal is often more enigmatic and creepy than any psychosomatic symptom could ever be. In accounting for why this might be, it is helpful to turn to an influential interpreter of Freud, the French psychoanalyst Jacques Lacan. For Lacan, what is ultimately at stake in hysteria is a kind of turning of the tables on the social order. In the face of implacable contradictory demands, the hysteric effectively makes a demand of her own—the demand to know what the social order really wants from her.

Lacan believes that this implacable question—"*What do you want from me?*"—is potentially revolutionary in its implications, because it cannot finally be answered. In particular cases, hysterics can be brought to a certain rapprochement with the social order, but any instance of hysterical questioning threatens to spiral out of control, revealing the inherent incompleteness of the social order: the final impossibility of its task of managing the unruliness of human desire.

The perversion of the social order

In our terms, it is easy to see the creepiness at work in hysteria. The relation to sexuality is clear, insofar as it is ultimately on women's bodies, their existence as sexual beings, that the social order's conflicting demands converge. Hysteria in its classical form was clearly invasive and displaced, insofar as it represented the body's attempt to enter the social order and speak, and it was enigmatic and excessive insofar as the psychosomatic symptom persisted without any medical cause and eluded all rational explanation.

The contemporary version, which better expresses the questioning that Lacan perceives at the heart of hysteria, bears those same traits to an even more radical degree. It is not merely displaced from its proper realm, because there is no place for it from the start. It is inherently displaced, a displacement that exists before the place for it. This means that it is not excessive in comparison with some standard, but is inherently excessive in itself, beyond or before any measure. It is irreducibly enigmatic for the same reason, existing by definition beyond the ability to be articulated in recognizable social terms. And it is more than simply invasive of the home or even the body: it is the very invasion of the body into the social expectations we call home.

We could therefore think of hysteria as a way of *creeping out the social order itself.* And just as in the case of the individual psyche, the social order is only susceptible to being creeped out due to the creepiness it carries within itself. Under normal circumstances, the social order appears to be obsessive in structure, opting for certain acceptable desires while repressing or excluding others. Yet from the hysteric's perspective, the most salient fact about the social order is the way it is continually setting us up to fail, so that it can even seem that the social order *needs* transgression and the illicit, creepy enjoyment that it provides. The social order's wink and nod of unofficial permission toward our creepy indulgences simultaneously makes social constraints more bearable *and* binds us more closely to the social order insofar as it makes those creepy indulgences possible. In short, the hysteric is uniquely positioned to see that the pervert has a point. All "normal" subjects contain an element of the perverse: hence the attractiveness of the perverse strategy for the obsessive.

Under the pressure of hysterical questioning, then, the social order reveals its perverse face—the fact that it runs on transgression, that it gets off on creepy violations. Few shows stage this perverse dynamic as dramatically as *Scandal*. Created by Shondra Rhimes, the show is a heavily fictionalized account of the work of Judy Smith, a former press aide to George Bush, Sr, who went on to run a crisis management firm. It stars Kerry Washington as Olivia Pope, a powerful D.C. "fixer" who was both campaign manager and lover to President Fitzgerald Grant III ("Fitz"). It is truly unique as a primetime drama created and produced by an African-American woman, with a strong African-American female lead, but it maintains an almost improbable silence about race, only mentioning the fact that Olivia is black when it might pertain to Fitz's reelection prospects. Within the frame of the show, race is something that only "someone else" cares about.

The real focus of the show is on Olivia's struggles as a powerful woman. Given her line of work, one might expect her to be the type of cold sociopath so common in contemporary TV drama, but she is very emphatically a caretaker. This starts with the crisis management firm itself, which is a kind of Island of Misfit Toys, providing purpose and structure to people whose lives have been destroyed by violence and crime. Some are more or less pure victims, while others have been deeply damaged by the horrible acts that circumstances forced them to commit. Even more than the situations of her clients, it is this group that Olivia wants to somehow "fix," repeatedly claiming that their work offers a chance at redemption—or in her somewhat belabored imagery, that they are "gladiators" fighting for justice, the "white hats" in a town full of corruption.

This task proves to be more difficult than it might seem. This is particularly true in the case of Huck, a former military man who was coerced into joining B613, a secretive domestic spy agency that employed him as a torturer and hit man. Torture has been commonplace on American television since 9/11, yet it feels grotesque and out of place here—and that appears to have been the writers' conscious intention. I say this because *Scandal* is virtually unique in reflecting on the seductiveness and addictiveness of violence, whereas a show like *24* always presented it as a grim necessity. Huck even goes to a 12-step program to help him control his violent impulses.

Olivia knows about all of this, and yet she both induces Huck to torture and kill *and* assigns him to train a younger "gladiator," who herself becomes addicted to violence and is drawn into the circle of B613. Other shows might justify all this via overarching moral necessities, but Olivia is frequently defending openly evil characters and even covering up their crimes. Indeed, she is deeply complicit with all that is worst in her world. Her own father turns out to be the head of B613, which initially appears to be an extra-governmental conspiracy but is then revealed to be fully authorized by a secret act of Congress that empowers it to "defend the Republic" by any means necessary. And though she is universally regarded as a genius-level campaign manager, it turns out that Fitz's first election was rigged, with Olivia's full knowledge and reluctant approval—a crime that she continues to help cover up, even when other co-conspirators commit murder and frame innocent bystanders.

Why does she do all this? Is it out of love for Fitz? The two rekindle and break off their relationship at least twice every season, and at one point Fitz even offers to divorce his wife Mellie (a fascinating character in her own right) and leave behind his political career so that the two can get married and start a family. Olivia seems open to this idea, but ultimately rejects it, presumably because she has given up so much of her moral integrity for Fitz's career. Later he believes he might be able to pull off divorcing Mellie while still running for a second term. She initially plays along, but is then convinced that it would never work politically. Later he shows her the beautiful cabin he has purchased and renovated in Vermont, where they will presumably be able to retire together when he's out of office (and where he'll be mayor and she'll make jam and babies). Again, it's tempting, but proves impossible.

One begins to suspect that the very impossibility of the relationship is its primary appeal for Olivia. The ambiguous situation allows her to take care of him by giving him emotional and sexual support—and at times Mellie openly embraces the relationship for that very reason—and then she breaks it off for the sake of higher priorities. This is of a piece with her broader strategy in life, where her commitment to being a "white hat" allows her to engage in the most varied and even random series of actions and to ally promiscuously with virtually all of her one-time enemies.

In the end, Olivia deeply wants to do "the right thing," yet it turns out that "the right thing" is more of an open-ended question than a determinate ethic or cause. This is in part because of the profound moral corruption of her world, where seemingly everyone (including the president himself!) is capable of literal hands-on murder. Here the contrast with 24 is instructive. While 24's government corruption often extended up to the highest levels, and uncomfortable alliances with formerly evil characters were frequently necessary, Jack Bauer had one indisputable moral goal that overrode everything else: he had to stop the terrorist attack. Olivia has no such luxury—it's corruption all the way down.

Or perhaps I should say "all the way up," because the perverse social order is headed by a perverse power couple on par with that of *House of Cards*. In this case, Mellie clearly has the upper hand in the long-term struggle, even if her ongoing quest to exercise absolute power through her husband does suffer occasional setbacks. Like Claire Underwood, she seamlessly jumps from strategy to strategy, most notably by approving and even actively soliciting Olivia's involvement with Fitz at one moment and threatening to expose it the next.

We see the same inconsistency in Fitz himself, who seems alternately bored by and passionately committed to his political career, willing to destroy it one day and willing to kill to preserve it the next. In his case, though, it seems less like deft scheming than like impotent acting out, as though he's funda- mentally a bored child. And he is very emphatically a child (not simply "Jr," but "III") to an overpowering father who constantly derides him and even feels entitled to rape Mellie (an event that Mellie, like Claire, manages to turn to her own advantage). This reference to his father's expectations might therefore help lend some coherence to his apparent flailing: he gets off on violating everyone's expectations, but their expectations are constantly changing. Hence sometimes he has to be the super-competent and dutiful president to thumb his nose at people who didn't think he could handle it, and sometimes he has to threaten to throw it all away just to keep his admirers on their toes. The conflicting demands may make Fitz seem almost like a hysteric, but at bottom he's a pervert.

Early in the series, Olivia is able to throw herself into her job as a way of deferring all the impossible conflicts she is embroiled in, but the moral complicity at times paralyzes her with indecision, resulting in depressive episodes where she appears to "go on strike" in the face of all the competing demands. At the end of the most recent season, she takes it to the next level. Noticing that, despite her good intentions, all of the most heinous crimes and conspiracies nevertheless directly involve her, she decides that she just needs to escape—and so she boards a secret plane to assume a new identity in an undisclosed location. Olivia's moral questioning winds up exposing the unfixable problems in the social order she is continually called upon to fix, ultimately driving her to abandon it in the quest for some kind of individual freedom.

Escapism, as we have seen, is more the obsessive's fantasy than the true outcome of hysteria, though we can surely expect that Olivia's escape will turn out to be illusory (if only because the network has ordered another season of the show). Yet even if Olivia turns out not to be a model hysteric, the show itself certainly is. At every turn, the viewer is tormented by unanswerable questions: what does *Scandal* want from us? Are we supposed to root for Fitz, for Mellie, for Olivia? Are we supposed to hope that the election rigging isn't found out, that the bodies remain buried? If so, why? Does the show want us to be repulsed by the use of torture, or titillated?

One thing's for certain: it doesn't invite us to take joy in political manipulation for its own sake, in the style of *House of Cards*. Here political manipulation isn't a virtuoso performance, but a series of increasingly desperate stop-gap measures. Things are more likely to work out by sheer random coincidence than by design—as when Fitz wins reelection due to the sudden death of his son. It is less overtly criminal than his first stolen victory (though it turns out the B613 had him killed to influence the outcome), and yet it hardly seems like a triumph for democracy.

One of the most distinctive aspects of the show—its highly stylized, over-dramatic dialogue—helps to intensify this hysterical dynamic. Seemingly every exchange of words takes the form of an urgent rant, so that every character appears to be converging into a unified stream of high-strung dialogue. Fitz's victory and his defeat are both declared equally urgent, in literally the same tone and style. B613 is at once crucial to the survival of America and a criminal enterprise that must be stopped by all means necessary—again, two angles that are expressed with the exact same cadences and pacing. The viewer joins Olivia in being barraged by all the contradictory demands of this twisted social order, and like Olivia, the viewer finds no answer but to escape, either by turning off the TV or sighing with relief when the season is finally over.

Don't. Stop.

Olivia Pope is hardly the first TV hysteric to opt for escape. I noted in the chapter on perversion, for instance, that Lena Dunham's character in *Girls* seems to go through a "perverse phase" but ultimately to be a hysteric—and interestingly, the most recent season also depicts her on the verge of simply leaving her social scene in New York behind, escaping to a creative writing program in Iowa. Peggy Olsen and Joan Harris of *Mad Men* also plan various escape routes, as when Peggy leaves Don Draper's agency to find a more supportive mentor and Joan tries to escape from office life by getting married.

We can see this strategy's appeal when we see what typically happens to television hysterics. One thinks immediately of Skyler White or Carmella Soprano, both of whom are put into an impossible and ultimately inescapable position by their husbands. Both flail from one strategy to the next, and both "go on strike" in various ways. In the end, however, they've been set up. Not only are they doomed to fail, but they are doomed to be reviled by the men in the audience. In the context of white straight male culture, their hysterical provocation is a decidedly unwelcome intrusion, to the point where fans have often rooted for their deaths.

This violent rejection of hysteria is the flip side of the

idealized "transcendent" woman. If the latter indulges the fantasy of the woman as able to bear the full burden of social contradictions, the former envisions the total destruction of the woman as punishment for her failure to meet that impossible standard. In both cases, a creepy enjoyment is at play: in the first case, the pervert's fantasy of "bringing his penis to the dinner party" and attaining full enjoyment within the social order's bounds; and in the second, the superego's enjoyment of punishment, its creepy demand for transgression.

Turning to the psychic structures of the shows themselves, I would like to focus on a moment where every show confronts impossible, contradictory expectations that it can never meet: namely, the ending. Particularly interesting here are the endings of the "high quality cable drama," a highly self-reflective genre whose writers must feel considerable pressure to "make a statement" in the show's final moments. A few series try to bring the overarching narrative to a satisfying conclusion, tying up the loose ends and allowing for a final assessment of the character. This is the case, for example, with *Breaking Bad*, which allows the viewer the satisfaction of seeing Walter White succeed in securing his immortality as a legendary criminal. This type of ending is continuous with the perverse structure of the show, inviting the viewer to identify one last time with the hero's transgressive desire. Others are unwittingly poignant, as with the ending of *Deadwood*, which closes on a note of moral ambiguity that leaves space for hysterical questioning. Admittedly, the series was unexpectedly cancelled, so that we'll never know what the "real" ending would have been, but the hystericizing effect of the open-ended finale is nevertheless very real.

Perhaps the most interesting case is *The Sopranos*. If *Breaking Bad* ended precisely on schedule and *Deadwood* was tragically cut short, *The Sopranos* belongs in an ambiguous third category: a show that was denied its proper ending. David Chase initially planned for three seasons, which would culminate when Tony

Soprano's mother betrayed him by testifying against him in court. Unfortunately, however, the woman who played Tony's mother unexpectedly died before filming was complete, forcing them to abruptly change course (and piece together a partly CGI version of the actress in order to kill off her character within the show).

Hence viewers got their wish: a hated female character met her demise. Yet once that happened, there was no real reason to go on. The show devolved into a meandering soap opera for two seasons, during which time its popularity grew significantly even as it decreased in quality. The sixth and final season was even separated into two distinct "parts" that aired in different years, further extending the series' run (a trend that has unfortunately continued in the cases of *Breaking Bad* and now *Mad Men*).

In the first half, one can almost sense the writers' desire to escape from the monstrosity they have created. They stage a scene of family betrayal, much like that of their intended conclusion—but this time the traitor is Tony's elderly Uncle Junior, who is suffering from dementia and doesn't even know who Tony is. And like the show itself, Tony survives this missed encounter, spending much of the season on life support. Curiously, the writers supplement the inert persistence of their star by staging enigmatic dream sequences in which Tony imagines that he is a businessman who has lost his briefcase at a conference. It's as though the prospect of a normal, mediocre life is the nightmare from which he must awaken to reclaim his rightful throne as a mafia boss.

Tony has evoked this kind of scenario before, as he continually refers to the nightmare of "selling patio furniture." Yet why shouldn't Tony have gone into the patio furniture business? Why follow in his father's footsteps? Why fight so hard to join this club of dying, demented old men? The show invites us to question further: why does the mafia even still exist? We might be able to imagine rationalizations for its existence in previous eras. Perhaps once it was a stable structure of authority for those distant from formal state structures. Perhaps once it was a way of defending the interests of immigrant communities neglected and marginalized in American culture. But *today*? Even granting that those rationales once made sense, can we really claim that they still hold today?

There is thus an inner necessity in the fact that *The Sopranos* continued to persist beyond its own mandate, because it is a show about an institution that has persisted beyond its own mandate. More than that, though, it is a show about the persistence of white power as such, because Tony is fully ensconced in the suburban world of McMansions and the meritocratic approach to childrearing that lands his daughter at Columbia University. For her part, Carmella is continually pictured reading *New York Times* bestsellers and wants nothing more than to become a participant in the bubble economy of the late 90s. And it's no wonder that the Sopranos fit so seamlessly into mainstream white culture, because their wealth depends on the same toxic blend of debt and violence that underwrites the contemporary social contract as a whole.

As the end approaches, the writers give us our fantasy, at least for a few episodes. Tony Soprano—who as a normal guy appears to be little more than your average fat, balding, pathetic sad sack—is revived and reclaims the animal energy that makes him so fascinating to watch. At great cost to himself and his friends, he defeats his enemies in a gruesome bloodbath that ends with a rival boss's head being satisfyingly crushed beneath the tire of his SUV.

In the last few scenes of the final episode, Tony is again haunted by the specter of the trial that his mother's death denied him, and he will be deprived of that trial once again by one of the most famous and controversial scenes in television history. Tony arranges to meet his family for a meal at a diner, where he selects Journey's "Don't Stop Believin'" on the jukebox. An elaborate tableau then unfolds, rich with religious imagery. Characters' actions begin to synchronize with the music, and all the while we notice a mysterious figure in a Members Only jacket, always just out of focus. We watch Meadow, the last of the family to arrive, struggle to fit into a tight parking space, and as Tony looks up — presumably at Meadow, but perhaps at an FBI agent there to arrest him, or an assassin (the Members Only guy?) — the music abruptly halts on the word "stop," and the screen cuts to black.

This scene rewards repeated viewings, and it has been subject to endless interpretations. Ultimately, though, I believe that all the symbolism, including the Members Only guy, is irreducibly ambiguous and actively misleading. If the writers had wanted to show us Tony's fate, they could have done so directly — all of our feverish attempts to string together the details into a coherent whole tells us more about our own desires than about what "really" happened to Tony. By concluding so abruptly, they are not simply denying us fulfillment, but asking us what we want out of Tony and out of the show as a whole. Why are we watching? *What do we want?*

Perhaps we can even read Chase and the other writers as having been hystericized by the demands of an audience that insisted on watching a show about an obsolete institution that was itself already past its prime by the time most of them started watching. And in true hysterical fashion, they finally went on strike, refusing all the competing demands. In that unexpected fade to black — which had many viewers feverishly checking to see if their TV was broken — *The Sopranos* is telling us: "Okay, if you sick creeps won't turn this off, I'll do it for you."

The creepiness of all flesh

At some points during my work on this project, I was tempted to end here, claiming that the entire ensemble of white straight male pop-cultural trends I was diagnosing — awkward humor, sociopathic anti-heroes, and overt creepiness — needed to take a cue from *The Sopranos* and just *stop*. This feeling was most intense when I finished the recent season of *Louie*, but it has never completely left me. Though I deeply love many of the shows I've been analyzing in this series, above all *Curb Your Enthusiasm* and *Mad Men*, it is hard to deny that these trends more often hit the mediocre level of *Family Guy* or *Dexter*. Surely, I thought, it's time for white straight men to step aside and let someone, *anyone*, have a chance!

At other times, I wanted to gesture toward some kind of radical social alternative just over the horizon. The temptation was greatest just after I watched *Her* and was struck by the way that it transcended the perverse Manic Pixie trope in the direction of a kind of utopia. This is not simply because of the refusal to reproduce the monogamous couple in Theodore and Amy, though that is an important element. More decisive for this reading of the film is the fact that Samantha is not simply imitating male roles and attitudes. Rather, she is experimenting with a genuinely new and unprecedented form of relating and communicating, one that is barely comprehensible from the perspective of our usual way of looking at the world. This development of a completely different way of being takes place incredibly rapidly, as the events of the film seem to take at most a year to unfold. Theodore and Amy, along with the rest of humanity, may not know exactly how to respond, but one thing is certain: they can't simply fall back on the old models.

It seems clear to me now that both options — the rejection of and the transcendence of pop-cultural trends — represented the same obsessive fantasy of a complete break between creepiness and the social order. Yet from the very beginning of my study of popular culture, I have implicitly acknowledged that you can't have one without the other. In *Awkwardness*, I claimed that awkwardness does not simply arise out of the violation or breakdown of social norms, but instead that awkwardness comes first and social norms represent our attempt to cope with it. At that time, entrapped as I was within the obsessive frame of white male awkwardness, I didn't have a good reason why that should be the case. If we now recognize awkwardness as arising out of the subject's self-creeping-out, the subject's own anxiety in the face of the unruliness of desire, we can recognize social norms as an attempt to channel and regulate that desire.

Yet given the intrinsically contradictory nature of desire itself, there's no way for any social order to account for and manage everything. There is always an unruly remainder that escapes from social control—a remainder that is from one perspective produced by social forces insofar as it is reacting to their demands, and yet from another perspective gives us a window into the self-creeping that gave rise to that social order in the first place. It is this remainder that is revealed in radical hysterical questioning, and once that questioning allows us to see the inherent creepiness of desire, we can see the way it "stains" the social order itself, providing little outlets, little "stashes" of forbidden desire that help to make social constraints bearable.

Creepiness points toward the ultimate breakdown of the social order at the same time as it accounts for its origin and its present hold on its members. Creepiness is thus the past, present, and future of human society: its eternal precondition, its eternal motor, and its eternal obstacle.

The inescapable and therefore universal nature of creepiness is not, however, the final word. There is also the question of the contingent, historical structures that we build in our ongoing attempt to cope with our inherent creepiness. If we concede that we will always creep ourselves out and therefore will always need some form of social order to help us manage our creepiness, we do not therefore concede that the social structure of the patri-archal middle class must always be with us.

I have claimed that the social order presupposed by white straight male popular culture oscillates between obsession and perversion. Now I would like to push further and claim that

what unites these two otherwise seemingly very different structures is their rejection of hysteria. The obsessive strategy rejects
hysteria insofar as hysteria reveals that the social order is necessarily tied up with creepiness. The perverse strategy, conversely,
rejects hysteria insofar as hysteria reveals the necessary lack in
the social order—in other words, its failure to attain the fullness
of creepiness.

On one level, then, the two seem to be polar opposites insofar
as one wants total creepiness and the other wants no creepiness
at all. Yet on a deeper level, both gestures are correlative insofar
as they both reject hysteria's message that the social order can
never be self-sufficient or self-contained. Psychosis may seem
like a possible escape from this dynamic for the individual, but
from this perspective, we can also see psychosis as a variation on
the theme: a recoil from reality that attempts to build a self-sufficient, self-contained "little world."

There is only one alternative, and that is to *persist in hysteria*,
to sustain the gap it opens up in the social order rather than
letting it collapse into the illusory self-enclosure of obsession or
perversion. This cannot simply mean setting up new rules that
will account for all that the current order excludes, which would
mean falling prey to the obsessive temptation, and neither can it
take the perverse form of subverting and violating social norms
for its own sake.

A small example of the kind of thing I mean can be found,
perhaps unexpectedly, in the use of nudity in *Girls*. Initially, I
said, her nudity was aggressively perverse, but as Lena
Dunham's character moves beyond her perverse indulgences in
later episodes, her nudity takes on a variety of new roles. For
instance, one scene depicts her getting dressed in the morning
after a shower, demonstrating her high level of comfort with her
live-in boyfriend. Other nude scenes highlight her vulnerability
or other emotional states—but none of them seem to have the
primary goal of sexually titillating the viewer, nor (as earlier) of

violating their normal expectations of sexual titillation. It's as though the show's excessive and aggressive use of nudity early on had somehow "de-activated" the customary pop-cultural use of female nudity, opening up a space for a more thorough exploration of what nudity could mean as part of the emotional landscape of a scene.

This shift would likely have been much more difficult to pull off for a woman who conformed more closely to conventional standards of attractiveness, who would necessarily be much more invested in the social expectations that have enshrined her as a great beauty. Another example indicates that there is a kind of advantage in this apparent disadvantage. I am thinking of Melissa McCarthy's character in *Bridesmaids*. Given that McCarthy's weight disqualifies her as a desirable sexual object according to the standards of pop culture, her frank sexuality is presented as incongruous and thus humorous. If this character appeared in an Adam Sandler movie, that would be the end of the story. Yet unlike so many of her peers, this character had the good fortune to appear in a movie written by a woman, and it is gradually revealed that she has a satisfying sex life and a fulfilling career—indeed, she appears to be the only truly healthy woman in the film and emerges as a mentor to her friends.

Both examples show what happens when hysteria shifts from being a protest to being a lifestyle. In the case of Olivia Pope (at least so far), the hysterical gesture is ultimately a purely negative one: "I'll never be what they want, so I might as well just give up." For Lena Dunham and Melissa McCarthy, by contrast, that initially negative gesture is transmuted into a productive one: "I'll never be what they want, so screw it, I might as well be what I am." This stance includes the attractive freedom of the psychotic, but without its fragility, and it gives us access to the confidence of the pervert without its destructive reliance on transgression for transgression's sake. Finally, the hysteric is still able to make provisional use of social norms, but without the rigid desperation that characterizes the obsessive stance. Hysteria acknowledges where we are now, but recognizes that we will not always remain here—and views that openness and uncertainty as more a promise than a threat.

The power of hysteria is the power of open possibilities, and hence wherever possibilities are opening up, there is an approach toward hysteria. The obsessive characters in *The Royal Tenenbaums* and *Moonrise Kingdom*, for instance, are moving toward a hysterical stance of open-ended questioning and exploration as they move toward a more livable approach to life. Most dramatically, in his bold gesture of escaping from his psychotic enclosure and reestablishing contact with reality, Don Draper makes a radical leap from psychosis into hysteria. He has attempted to escape before—by starting the new agency, by marrying his seemingly perfect second wife—but those escapes still left him trapped inside the illusion of total control. In the end, he escapes from the will to control and hence from the very desire to escape. Life isn't perfect for him, as he faces considerable disappointment and even humiliation, but for the first time he finds genuine satisfaction in his work and genuine connection with his long-time friend and mentor, his young protégés, and his daughter.

Sustained hysteria means acknowledging the fact that there will never be a perfect solution to the fundamentally unfixable problem of human creepiness. And once we let go of that fantasy of perfection and fullness, what previously seemed to be a tragic flaw appears instead as an opportunity and even an invitation: to live, to enjoy, to forge new connections, to find new ways of shaping our shared lives together. I have said that for the psychotic, all things are possible—until nothing is. We might say that for the hysteric, that most radical of creeps, not everything is possible—but anything might become so.

Contemporary culture has eliminated both the concept of the public and the figure of the intellectual. Former public spaces – both physical and cultural – are now either derelict or colonized by advertising. A cretinous anti-intellectualism presides, cheerled by expensively educated hacks in the pay of multinational corporations who reassure their bored readers that there is no need to rouse themselves from their interpassive stupor. The informal censorship internalized and propagated by the cultural workers of late capitalism generates a banal conformity that the propaganda chiefs of Stalinism could only ever have dreamt of imposing. Zer0 Books knows that another kind of discourse – intellectual without being academic, popular without being populist – is not only possible: it is already flourishing, in the regions beyond the striplit malls of so-called mass media and the neurotically bureaucratic halls of the academy. Zer0 is committed to the idea of publishing as a making public of the intellectual. It is convinced that in the unthinking, blandly consensual culture in which we live, critical and engaged theoretical reflection is more important than ever before.

ZERO BOOKS

If this book has helped you to clarify an idea, solve a problem or extend your knowledge, you may like to read more titles from Zero Books. Recent bestsellers are:

Capitalist Realism Is there no alternative?
Mark Fisher
An analysis of the ways in which capitalism has presented itself as the only realistic political-economic system.
Paperback: November 27, 2009 978-1-84694-317-1 $14.95 £7.99.
eBook: July 1, 2012 978-1-78099-734-6 $9.99 £6.99.

Wandering Who? The A study of Jewish identity politics
Gilad Atzmon
An explosive unique crucial book tackling the issues of Jewish Identity Politics and ideology and their global influence.
Paperback: September 30, 2011 978-1-84694-875-6 $14.95 £8.99.
eBook: September 30, 2011 978-1-84694-876-3 $9.99 £6.99.

Clampdown Pop-cultural wars on class and gender
Rhian E. Jones
Class and gender in Britpop and after, and why 'chav' is a feminist issue.
Paperback: March 29, 2013 978-1-78099-708-7 $14.95 £9.99.
eBook: March 29, 2013 978-1-78099-707-0 $7.99 £4.99.

Quadruple Object, The
Graham Harman
Uses a pack of playing cards to present Harman's metaphysical system of fourfold objects, including human access, Heidegger's indirect causation, panpsychism and ontography.
Paperback: July 29, 2011 978-1-84694-700-1 $16.95 £9.99.

Weird Realism Lovecraft and Philosophy
Graham Harman
As Hölderlin was to Martin Heidegger and Mallarmé to Jacques Derrida, so is H.P. Lovecraft to the Speculative Realist philosophers.
Paperback: September 28, 2012 978-1-78099-252-5 $24.95 £14.99.
eBook: September 28, 2012 978-1-78099-907-4 $9.99 £6.99.

Sweetening the Pill or How We Got Hooked on Hormonal Birth Control
Holly Grigg-Spall
Is it really true? Has contraception liberated or oppressed women?
Paperback: September 27, 2013 978-1-78099-607-3 $22.95 £12.99.
eBook: September 27, 2013 978-1-78099-608-0 $9.99 £6.99.

Why Are We The Good Guys? Reclaiming Your Mind From The Delusions Of Propaganda
David Cromwell
A provocative challenge to the standard ideology that Western power is a benevolent force in the world.
Paperback: September 28, 2012 978-1-78099-365-2 $26.95 £15.99.
eBook: September 28, 2012 978-1-78099-366-9 $9.99 £6.99.

Truth about Art, The Reclaiming quality
Patrick Doorly
The book traces the multiple meanings of art to their various sources, and equips the reader to choose between them.
Paperback: August 30, 2013 978-1-78099-841-1 $32.95 £19.99.

Bells and Whistles More Speculative Realism
Graham Harman
In this diverse collection of sixteen essays, lectures, and interviews Graham Harman lucidly explains the principles of

Speculative Realism, including his own object-oriented philosophy.

Paperback: November 29, 2013 978-1-78279-038-9 $26.95 £15.99.
eBook: November 29, 2013 978-1-78279-037-2 $9.99 £6.99.

Towards Speculative Realism: Essays and Lectures
Graham Harman
These writings chart Harman's rise from Chicago sportswriter to co founder of one of Europe's most promising philosophical movements: Speculative Realism.

Paperback: November 26, 2010 978-1-84694-394-2 $16.95 £9.99.
eBook: January 1, 2010 978-1-84694-603-5 $9.99 £6.99.

Meat Market Female flesh under capitalism
Laurie Penny
A feminist dissection of women's bodies as the fleshy fulcrum of capitalist cannibalism, whereby women are both consumers and consumed.

Paperback: April 29, 2011 978-1-84694-521-2 $12.95 £6.99.
eBook: May 21, 2012 978-1-84694-782-7 $9.99 £6.99.

Translating Anarchy The Anarchism of Occupy Wall Street
Mark Bray
An insider's account of the anarchists who ignited Occupy Wall Street.

Paperback: September 27, 2013 978-1-78279-126-3 $26.95 £15.99.
eBook: September 27, 2013 978-1-78279-125-6 $6.99 £4.99.

One Dimensional Woman
Nina Power
Exposes the dark heart of contemporary cultural life by examining pornography, consumer capitalism and the ideology of women's work.

Paperback: November 27, 2009 978-1-84694-241-9 $14.95 £7.99.

eBook: July 1, 2012 978-1-78099-737-7 $9.99 £6.99.

Dead Man Working
Carl Cederstrom, Peter Fleming
An analysis of the dead man working and the way in which
capital is now colonizing life itself.
Paperback: May 25, 2012 978-1-78099-156-6 $14.95 £9.99.
eBook: June 27, 2012 978-1-78099-157-3 $9.99 £6.99.

Unpatriotic History of the Second World War
James Heartfield
The Second World War was not the Good War of legend. James
Heartfield explains that both Allies and Axis powers fought for
the same goals - territory, markets and natural resources.
Paperback: September 28, 2012 978-1-78099-378-2 $42.95 £23.99.
eBook: September 28, 2012 978-1-78099-379-9 $9.99 £6.99.

Find more titles at www.zero-books.net